GROWING
SUCCULENT PLANTS

To my wife and illustrator, Heather Graham, for her help and patience, and her excellent drawings

GROWING
SUCCULENT
PLANTS

Victor Graham

TIMBER PRESS
Portland, Oregon

Illustrations by Heather Graham
and photographs by the author

ISBN: 0-88192-036-3

Text and illustrations © Victor Graham 1987

First published in the USA in 1987 by
Timber Press,
9999 S. W. Wilshire,
Portland, Oregon 97225
USA

Printed and bound in Great Britain

Contents

•1•
The Appeal
of Succulent Plants

There are many reasons why succulent plants are becoming so popular. Living things from another part of the world will always have the special appeal of the unusual, whether they are plants, birds, fishes or other exotics. However much we may care for our native flora and fauna, we must have dull minds if they do not respond to something new and different.

Yet there is more to succulents than their strangeness. Bizarre they may be in shape and form, but they are beautiful in their oddity and it is this quality which endears them to so many greenhouse gardeners. Whether it is the varied colours and textures of leaves and bodies, the unique manner of adaptation and growth, or the brightness of flowers which have no counterpart in other regions of the plant kingdom, there is always something in a collection of succulents to attract the eye and intrigue the imagination. What is more, there is no one season for these fascinating plants; at any time of the year some will be growing and some resting, some budding up and others ripening their seed pods. When the world outside the greenhouse begins to die down for winter, many succulents will be stirring themselves and preparing to delight us with their colour and their flowers. These include the tiny 'mimicry' plants from South Africa, aeoniums from the Canary Islands, euphorbias from Madagascar – and many others among the vast range of succulents now in cultivation.

Beginners who visit a mature collection of succulents are sometimes surprised to see so many of the plants in bloom, whatever the time of year. They should not be. Most succulent plants should flower regularly and annually, if they are being grown correctly. Even if grown from seed, some species, such as the dwarf mesembryanthemums and one or two stepaliads will bloom in their first year. It is quite possible, whatever legend says to the contrary, to have cacti in flower before they are much over a year old. Various species of terrestrial cacti, mammillarias (some), rebutias (many), and turbinicarpus (most) should do so, and occasionally species from other genera may prove as precocious. The belief that flowers may be expected only every seven, twenty, or even every one hundred years is equally nonsensical. Most succulent plants should be in bloom every year.

During the last decade or so a much greater understanding of succulent plants has been gained, much of it due to the increase in their popularity. This understanding has led to their being grown and flowered more successfully, and much more easily. A number of excellent, specialist monographs have appeared, often written by botanists and collectors who have spent years in the field, in one continent or another. Gradually it has become possible to put together new information concerning the behaviour of succulents of all sorts in their natural habitats, particularly the more recent introductions. The results have been illuminating. No longer treated as 'desert' plants, which was once the fate destined for all succulents, whatever their real nature, the specimens in our greenhouses are now flourishing as they should do. Intelligent observation of their habits and growth in cultivation has helped to develop better ways of caring for them, and more effective ways of assisting conservation or propagating them. Many of these newer techniques are included in this volume. It is hoped that, with their aid, succulent growers will be able to cultivate successfully and enjoy these intriguing plants from the world's wilder places.

1in (2.5cm)

Aloinopsis rosulata, from the Cape Province, grows easily from seed and will produce its shining, yellow flowers in midwinter. A large pot is needed to accommodate the thongy roots. Alternatively, they may be partly raised above soil level and the species grown as a caudiciform succulent.

•2•
Succulent Plants
in the Wild

Desert plants?

Succulent plants have a widespread distribution about the world and are found in a variety of different environments, both dry and wet. Yet, in spite of the persisting belief that they do so, very few of them actually live in the desert, not even most cacti. Why the mistake continues to be made is not too hard to understand. In various dry parts of our planet, the inhabitants refer to the place where they live as 'the desert'. This is particularly true in the south-western United States, the home of so many cacti and other xerophytic plants. However, this so called desert is nearly always semi-desert and the difference between these two types of natural habitat is considerable. It is of particular importance to gardeners, and to the succulent plants which we grow.

There are few succulents to be found in real deserts; such places are simply too tough for them. In real deserts the plants to be found are usually annuals and semi annuals, whose seeds germinate when the rains return. They enjoy a brief life during the ensuing rainy season and then die, leaving their own seed behind them to germinate in its turn when the next rainy season arrives. This may not be for a period of years. Succulents, on the other hand, store water against the stress of dry seasons, and this water must be available to begin with.

Ecologists usually define a desert as a place where the annual average rainfall is 10in (25cm) or less. In semi-deserts, however, the annual rainfall may be twice as much. In real deserts long periods of drought cause the few species of cactus and dwarf desert mesems such as the lithops and conophytums to follow the annual plants into oblivion and die out completely. They survive as seed, only until rain falls again.

Even in semi-deserts succulents may have a hard time of it if they are to cope with the heat and the desiccating effect of hot winds. Successful succulent growth is nearly always helped by the presence of nearby, sheltering trees, scrub vegetation or rocks. Without these few succulents would survive, especially in their seedling stage.

The tall cacti which are seen frequently in Western films, and the superficially similar African succulents like the tree aloes and tree euphorbias, stand in very exposed positions. Nevertheless, when they were tiny seedlings and even young plants, they were certainly nursed by the shade and humid conditions provided by parent plants, or by the bushy scrub growth which still, in the majority of cases, surrounds their bases. Some cacti and some other succulents have adapted to real desert conditions, frequently by evolving into miniature species, which are usually very slow growing. It should be noted however, that even the Namib, a true desert and one of the cruellest environments on this planet, enjoys regular, dense fogs, which roll in from the Atlantic during the winter months. Only these – for rain falls seldom – permit a wide variety of succulent plants to survive there.

There are two other points concerning deserts and semi-deserts which are of great importance to all of us who grow succulent plants. First: desert climates undergo very wide changes of temperature during a twenty-four-hour cycle (even 100°F, 37.5°C is not unknown) and this invariably produces a heavy precipitation of dew during the night. When the nocturnal fall in temperature is extreme the dew becomes frost. Second: desert soils are poor only because they are deficient in humus, but this does not mean that the plants which grow in such areas are deprived of nourishment. Desert soils are rich in mineral content and have only to be moistened by rain or dew for this to become effective.

Rain forest succulents

If real deserts are the driest habitats, then tropical rain forests are the wettest. Newcomers to our hobby are sometimes bewildered when they find out that so many of our plants come from the steamy wet jungles of the tropics. Even here where each year as much as 150cm (60in) of rain may fall, it is possible for some plants to suffer from water shortage. The truth is that rain-forest succulents are epiphytic by nature; that is, they lead non-terrestrial lives above the forest floor, unable to reach what may well be a plentiful supply of water and food available to the terrestrial plants below them. Tropical jungles are often rich in succulent plant life. One could limit a whole collection to them and still find that there are simply too many to collect.

Dry forests are to rain forests what deserts are to semi-deserts. The principal difference is that rain forests do not have a really dry season, while dry forests enjoy a period during the year when it is far less humid. Dry forest succulents are more likely to be terrestrial or semi-terrestrial in their habit. This means that many of them are able to benefit from the nourishment of moist, humus-rich soil at most times of the year. Dry seasons are normally short and, when they occur, it is common for heavy dews or fogs to compensate for the lack of rain.

One further point is worth remembering. The difference between day-time and night-time temperatures in rain forests is much smaller than that usually found in desert areas. The luxuriant tree canopy, a feature of the tropical rain forest, modifies the daily change and keeps the days cooler and the nights warmer. Dry forests, which are more or less open to the sky, will have warmer days and cooler nights than the rain forest.

Droughtland succulents

The habitats discussed so far are real ones, each of them described by a word familiar to geographers, climatologists and other specialists. However, most succulent plants do not originate in such extreme environ-

1in (2.5cm)

Agave victoria-reginae, a beautiful, slow growing species from Mexico. It is usually seen as a solitary rosette, but some forms grow into clumps. Among collectors this agave is highly prized for its bold markings and small size.

ments: they are found in a wide range of different places between such extremes.

Some of these more average habitats are tropical, some are temperate. A few are sub arctic, eg the alpine stations where such succulents as sedums and sempervivums live. Other habitats may be insular, maritime or continental; some mountainous and some at sea level. The only natural phenomenon which is common to all such regions of the world where succulent plants are found, is the period of dryness or water shortage which they all experience. This may be an annual one; it may be part of a longer cycle, or it may be an irregular occurrence. Drought periods may be long or short but, generally speaking, these habitats fare better than the desert areas, as the adapted forms of the inhabitant species indicate. In short, these droughtland areas have fairly regular dry periods which are neither too long nor too severe.

Our hobby badly needs a simple way of describing and grouping together the many species of succulents which live in these many, non-extreme habitats. This is particularly important, as by far the greatest number of succulent plants now to be found in cultivation originate from them. Such words as savannah, scrub, thornbush and so on will not do. They are, strictly speaking applicable to particular areas of the world, each of which has its own plant life. The word which we want must be capable of being used to describe any or all of these special habitats, and therefore to define the sort of cultivation which will be successful for all, or at least the great majority, of the succulent plants which are native to them. I began to use the expression 'droughtland' some time ago, and the adoption of this word by an increasing number of growers would seem to justify it. Until a better word comes along, this one will serve well enough for our purpose.

For gardening purposes it is both reasonable and practical to group droughtland plants together. Even if their original homes differ, they will generally settle down to one method of cultivation and thrive upon it. Of course there are always tricky plants. There are others, too, which obstinately refuse to produce their flowers, at least with any consistency or regularity. But, in spite of occasional setbacks, the basic method which will be suggested for cultivating droughtland succulents should suit most of them well enough. Gardeners who have the time, the skill or the patience, or who have a specialised interest in some of these plants, may modify the principles as they choose.

•3•
Where to Grow Succulents

Most succulent plants are not sufficiently resistant to cold to be considered hardy in any areas where frost occurs. Nearly all sempervivums, a number of sedums, and even one or two cacti, will cope with cold winters, but in general it is best to provide winter protection for all plants in the collection.

A few other true succulents may be tried out of doors and some will survive several winters under shelter. It is good practice to put plants out of doors during the warmer months. Not only does it benefit the plants but it gives their owner a chance to give the greenhouse its annual cleaning. Epiphytic plants, never ones for excessive heat, seem particularly to enjoy this yearly holiday. Hung up in the cool shade of a loggia amid the roses, or half hidden among the leaves of orchard trees, they will thrive in the broken light and enjoy every breeze and shower.

In a good year, with a warm summer and a long autumn, it is safe to leave plants out in the open until the first frosts threaten. Then no time should be lost in bringing them back into the safety of their winter home.

The greenhouse

A greenhouse is usually recommended for growing succulent plants in, but many serious collectors are beginning to ask themselves if it is the best environment. In the cooler countries succulents need winter warmth, but not too much heat in summer. A greenhouse is an extremely inefficient structure and the typical small greenhouse, which heats up and loses heat so quickly, shows this lack of efficiency at its greatest. A greenhouse may in fact be relied upon to keep most of our plants too cold in winter and too hot in summer. The summer problem may be solved fairly easily by providing very good ventilation and shading. The winter problem can be overcome by various types of heating, though it is annoying to heat a structure which will quickly lose its expensive warmth. Nevertheless, greenhouses are pleasant places for the gardener to be in during much of the year, especially if they are artificially lit, and I imagine that they will be with us for some time to come. It will be best, therefore, to consider these first of all, before discussing alternative ways of growing succulents.

Manufacturers and salesmen always advise that a greenhouse should be situated in the sunniest part of the garden, and to a great extent this is reasonable advice, especially in urban areas where there may be other buildings, trees or hedges close by. However, where none of these nuisances exist, it would be wise to keep one's greenhouse out of the sunniest position, which will also be the hottest one. A situation which provides a little shade, especially if this comes at midday, will help to keep the temperature down and prevent cherished plants from being scorched.

Most succulents love as much light as we can give them but even the real desert species do not enjoy too much sunlight under glass. It must not be forgotten that succulents in their natural habitat are seldom in still air. Even on the hottest days there will usually be a little movement around them. Most wild plants will probably be kept cooler by the shade of other vegetation or a rock or boulder. In the greenhouse, our plants are usually living in trapped air, unless ventilation is very efficient or a fan is being used.

Specimens may also suffer from a disadvantage which affects all pot plants under glass – the pots themselves. On warm days these can heat up rapidly, especially if they are plastic. It is not at all uncommon for the temperature to rise to nearly 40°C (over 100°F) in a small, free-standing greenhouse, on a hot summer day. No succulents appreciate such heat, especially if their roots are being slowly cooked.

If you do decide to buy a greenhouse it will need as many ventilators as possible, both along its roof and its side walls. Do not be persuaded that cacti and succulents need as much heat as possible. Ideally, you will need an 'alpine house,' a greenhouse with continuous ventilation provided along the whole length of the roof and the walls. On a still day in summer you will sometimes need all the ventilation you can achieve, and a good fan into the bargain.

Even in winter a sunny spell may be a hazard, especially for those succulents which are dormant, unless care is taken with ventilation. Automatic vents are an excellent way to avoid accidental scorching and would have prevented damage to my own plants several years ago when I was prevented from returning home one cold February. Many of my

1in (2.5cm)

Kalanchoe pumila, from Central Madagascar, grows to about 8in (20cm) in height. It has white, pruinose leaves and red-violet flowers. Semi-shade, careful watering (taking care not to wet and mark the foliage) and a winter temperature which does not fall below 45°F (7.5°C) will suit it.

plants were dormant at this time and, without ventilation, unexpected bright sunshine badly scorched a number of resting, terrestrial cacti on the south side of the greenhouse.

For most succulent plants, with the possible exception of the South African mesembryanthemums and the terrestrial cacti, a lean-to greenhouse or a glass-roofed conservatory will probably provide the best solution to the problem of growing succulent plants in cold countries like our own (unless you prefer to keep your collection indoors). If you can, choose a site which has a southern or western exposure. One which faces east or north is still usable, but not so good. In summer as much ventilation as possible will still be needed, but if the back wall of a lean-to is a house wall, it will do much to keep it warmer in winter. If local building regulations permit, it may be possible to have a door or window in this back wall, so that some heat may reach the plants from the house. Such a wall is also useful for growing and displaying hanging or trailing succulents.

Some enthusiasts are now beginning to think that it might be better and cheaper to dispense with a glass structure altogether for growing tender plants. In some parts of the world the winter climate makes it impossible to heat such a building, and yet succulent plant collectors still manage to grow and flower their plants by using artificial light in a heated basement or spare room. Rather than using a greenhouse, it will be far cheaper, even in mild climates, to heat and light a well insulated room in the house, or even to buy a wooden shed or garage and insulate it. Such methods have already become quite common for growing African violets successfully. If sufficient alternative lighting is provided succulents do not appear to miss the more natural light of the sun.

Only the accumulated experience of cultivators who do use artificial light for their plants will tell us just how much of it should be provided. So far, little research has been carried out on non-commercial subjects. If, however, the decision is taken to use this method of growing, it will probably be best to choose fluorescent lamps for illumination, as they have several advantages. There is a good choice of colour, the light is evenly spread and they are economical to run. Some fluorescent lamps are sold specially for horticultural use, but they are much more expensive and do not appear to have any advantages. The difference in wavelength between the various colours of fluorescent lamps is of much less importance than the overall intensity of the light emitted. Two 'ordinary' fluorescent lamps would be more effective.

In the conservatory or greenhouse a fluorescent lamp or two will do much to cheer the plants up on dull winter days. For terrestrial cacti and mesems this extra light will be of as much benefit, perhaps more, than a high daytime temperature, especially for those plants which flower during our darker months. Even if it is used only on sunless days it would be worth the small expense of its installation.

The use of artificial light brings another advantage. Succulents grown with its help can be given a much more natural year. In general, in countries which are distant from the Equator, succulent plants are undoubtedly inhibited, not only by the shortness and dullness of winter days, but equally by long, summer days, with their short, warmish nights (a problem which will be referred to again). Automatic timers make it possible to programme longer, artificial days during the winter months. In the same way hens are kept laying at this time of year.

Succulents in the home

People sometimes ask what the difference is between house plants and succulents. Succulent plants are a group which share certain vegetable or botanical characteristics, the principal one being the ability to store food and water, in various ways, against times of shortage. House plants, on the other hand, may be quite unrelated as plants. They share a common description only because they are suitable for growing together in our homes. One sometimes hears it said of one of the greener, leafier succulents that 'it looks more like a house plant', and many true succulents occur naturally in the same localities as so-called house plants. Usually these localities are forested and, as a rule, the succulent species will be non-terrestrial, growing up above the 'house plants'. Quite clearly, if two plants grow naturally together they will be likely to enjoy each other's company in our houses, if certain precautions are taken.

The first and principal problem encountered when setting out to grow succulent plants indoors is to find enough light for them. They cannot have too much. For a while, succulents may put up with less light than they really need, especially if they are resting; but eventually they will begin to lose tone and colour, growth will etiolate and become atypical and a general decline will follow. Even so the poor things may linger on for years, the slow growers also being the slowest to die. Some succulents show an astonishing tenacity and hold on life which almost invites the non-caring treatment meted out to them. Because of this, beginners are not always aware that their plants are changing for the worse. It is a sound idea to check on condition occasionally and one of the best ways is to compare plants with illustrations of the same species in a good reference book.

Enough light for succulent plants (it cannot be stated too often) does not mean that they should be exposed to hot, strong sunlight. That can prove as lethal as too little light, especially for forest species. Each year it is inevitable that, as summer comes round, the popular gardening press will feature the same old articles, embodying the same old advice. All of them talk about 'that hot, sunny windowsill, where nothing else will grow' and then continue to recommend it as 'just the spot for your cacti' (with which, in articles of this sort, all other succulents are usually lumped). Unfortunately, if nothing else will grow in this sort of situation, it will almost certainly prove to be a most efficient death trap, even for cacti. One sometimes visits a house where a few miserable, scorched specimens are displayed on such a windowsill. Their owners have not thrown them out, having no idea that the plants are quite dead, as they often are. Everybody knows, of course, that cacti don't grow, never need repotting and hardly ever need water! 'They're supposed to look dead, aren't they?' Oh yes, that question is not unknown.

If they are growing as they should be, all succulent plants show it, except, just possibly when they are dormant. Desert plants are no exception. When they are actively growing their appearance will leave no doubt as to whether or not they are alive. If the light is sufficient the plant's body or leaves should display a flush of brighter colour or gleam with health. New leaf or stem growth may be emerging and show as a point of green life. Where the period of rest forces the specimen to live on its own reserves and wrinkle or protrude its ribs or angles, the growing period, with its food and water should fill these out and give the whole plant a tightly packed, well fed look.

A sunny window can be a very good place for a display of succulent plants – sometimes. First of all, plants should be chosen from those which live naturally in more barren environments. They are usually those with hard bodies or leaves and thus adapted to put up with hot, dry situations. The terrestrial cacti, most agaves and aloes, gasterias, haworthias (not the softer ones), sansevierias, and similar droughtlanders offer plenty of choice. Secondly, there should be a burglar-proof ventilator which can safely be left open when the house is empty. This precaution, especially if the room door is left open, will ensure that there is always a beneficial through movement of fresh air; no matter how hot the day turns out to be, the temperature will always be reduced. There are other safeguards. A net curtain or shade from a tree outside will help to protect succulents from extreme heat on a sunny windowsill.

All these suggestions apply to a really hot situation, which is usually south facing. Windowsills with other exposures are easier to manage, although those which face north should be reserved for species which do not suffer from a more or less sunless existence, unless artificial light can be installed. But, whatever the aspect, all succulents will fare better if they have a little fresh air to cheer them up.

In cooler situations the small epiphytes and jungle succulents will be perfectly contented and many should flower. Rhipsalis, hoyas and ceropegias, some euphorbias and members of the liliaceae are all most suitable. North-facing windows are the coldest ones and, during the winter months, their occupants will welcome a little heat, which could be provided by the radiator often fitted below such windows. Whatever the aspect of a window curtains must be drawn against the glass at night. Plants left in the cold pocket of air between curtains and glass will be very much at risk on a cold night. Double-glazing lessens the problem, as it does that of excessive heat during the daytime.

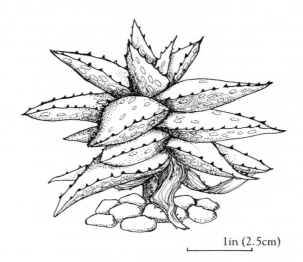

1in (2.5cm)

Aloe jucunda, a dwarf species from Somalia, which slowly forms a short stem and increases by making offsets. The hard, dark-green leaves are flecked with pale spots and the flowers, which may appear more than once during the year, are displayed in a simple raceme of pale-pink, cylindrical bells. The ease of growing and the beauty of the flowers make this a popular succulent in collections.

Imaginative gardeners should be able to find themselves other indoor situations for their plants, providing that the two essentials, light (natural or artificial) and warmth are present. There are few homes nowadays which get too cold at night for succulent plants.

One attractive way of growing and displaying a small collection of plants is to make a plant shelf or a plant corner – even the top of a cupboard or bookshelf would provide sufficient space. The base could be a watertight tray and this should be kept half or three-quarters full of grit, gravel, pebbles or a lightweight material such as peat where weight is a consideration. The prepared tray would act as a plungebed or standing area for pots of plants and would provide humidity, which would particularly benefit succulents of the epiphytic and rain-forest type.

Over the display, one or more fluorescent lamps should be fitted, preferably with a reflector, to throw more light downwards and concealed behind a pelmet. A further refinement could be the installation of a mirror behind the plants, or two set at right angles in the corner of a room, which would make a few plants look almost like a jungle.

It is quite possible to set plants directly into a tray of compost, giving the display a much more natural appearance. However, this can bring problems, although experienced growers may prefer the approach and use it with success. All indoor gardening of this sort is experimental, at least to begin with and a more flexible way of growing may bring fewer disappointments. Individually potted plants will give more scope for re-arrangement and those which do less well may be changed for others. They may also be knocked out of their pots easily and examined to see if there is a specific reason for their not thriving. Some plants, even if they are not victims of disease or pests, may simply not fit in with the majority, but require more or less water, more heat or light, and so on. All plants grown indoors will enjoy a summer holiday in the greenhouse or garden and, while they are on vacation, a completely different selection could occupy their winter home.

Bathrooms sometimes turn out to be very successful for indoor succulent plant growing and they provide a practical winter haven for the more tender species. Most modern bathrooms have their chills reduced by a radiator or towel rail, and a shelf fitted above this or behind the bath will accommodate a colourful display of such things as rhipsalis and lepismium, hoyas and ceropegias, cynanchums, dischidias, schlumbergeras and the like. Bromeliads will also give contrast to the display. Flowers may be expected from many of the species included in this list of plants and a light bathroom will encourage even more blooms.

Like bathrooms, kitchens are also extra humid at times and their moist atmosphere should not be wasted. Even a small shelf can be squeezed in somewhere for one or two favourite plants. The constant traffic in and out of both bathrooms and kitchens ensures that there is a continual change of air. Succulents exposed to cooking fumes and sooty deposits for very long should be washed off or sprayed occasionally to keep them as clean as possible.

Succulents in outdoor frames

Frames are sometimes recommended for the outdoor growing of various plants, succulents among them. There is no denying the fact that they have advantages, especially for such succulents as the dwarf mesems, desert cacti and other small, light-loving species, eg, the winter crassulas and anacampseros species of the Avonia section. All plants of this type need very little heat, if any, and it would be a simple matter to equip a garden frame with a heating cable, covering the frame on cold nights with a plastic tarpaulin or something similar to conserve a little heat. In these conditions, plants like those listed above will undoubtedly thrive, look really well in such a light situation and benefit from the airiness of their home. With some structures of this sort it is even possible to remove most of the glass panels completely for much of the year and even further improve the general situation. However, there is one snag: in winter, while the lucky occupants of the frame are enjoying a little protection, the unlucky gardener has to remain outside in rain, snow or biting wind while the plants are being serviced or inspected. Some gardeners are happy to make such a sacrifice, others prefer the compara- tive luxury of a greenhouse or conservatory. It is up to the grower to choose for himself.

•4•
How to Grow Succulents

Most of the succulent plants available today are reasonably easy to grow and to flower. Some, it must be admitted, are not, and these need all the skill and patience which experience can bring. Quite often these tricky species have little to recommend them beyond their rarity and the beginner will probably not come across such plants. If he does he should trust his own good taste and not be tempted by obscure names, even if they are fashionable ones. Few of these oddities can compete with some of the old favourites, which still take pride of place in the collections of real plant lovers.

As far as the general run of succulent plants is concerned (ie, those which are most often seen in collections, or which are obtainable from dealers or nurseries) the suggestions for cultivation outlined in the following pages should serve to grow them successfully. Where the proper treatment differs from this, for particular plants, it will be mentioned. Those plants which share certain needs in cultivation have been given sections of their own in a later chapter.

Composts

The choice between composts is far from easy. The increasing shortage of loam and the fact that peat harvesting and marketing is now a huge business has resulted in such a variety of brand names and different mixtures that the gardener is sometimes completely at a loss to know which is best for his particular purpose. Luckily, succulents are adaptable and will accept all sorts of growing mixtures, as long as these fulfil certain important requirements.

The usual preference today is for a loamless compost, and this is nearly always based on peat. These peat-based mixes may also contain such ingredients as sand or grit, or manufactured ones such as vermiculite or perlite. In addition, a quantity of artificial feed is added, to make up for the lack of nourishment which distinguishes these modern 'artificial'

1in (2.5cm)

Haworthia fouchei, from the southern Cape Province, belongs to the *Retusae* group of hawor-thias, which have blunt, recurved and transparent tips to the leaves. Good light is needed to keep the rosettes of this species tight.

composts from the older ones. A small amount of lime, in some form or other, is sometimes incorporated to counteract the natural acidity of some peats. Modern, commercial composts have several advantages. They are consistent in make-up (an important point), they are clean and sterile (though not always as completely as is claimed for them), and they are easy to buy. It is important to start with a neutral compost if possible, which may be modified for special purposes. Most of the reliable, popular mixtures are corrected to a pH of 7; but it is always worth checking to make sure. Information of this sort is often printed on the plastic sack itself, or included on an information sheet slipped inside it.

Loam-based composts are perfectly satisfactory, if a good one can be found, or the ingredients obtained for home mixing. Some experienced growers will, in fact, use nothing else. As well as loam these mixtures should contain sand or grit, peat or leafmould and a food ingredient, together with a small amount of ground chalk, used, as in the peat-type mixes, as a 'sweetener' to correct any excess acidity. The well known John Innes composts are of this type and are very good indeed. At least they were. Unfortunately, the John Innes Institute was responsible only for originating the formulae for the various 'J.I.' mixtures. It has no control whatsoever over the quality of the composts which are marketed under the name, and there are some very poor examples to be had.

There are other ingredients which are sometimes to be found in composts and there are even growers who seem to spend more time inventing magic mixes than growing plants in them. One book, in fact, which limited itself to the growing of cacti and which was widely read some twenty-five years ago, included recipes for nearly thirty different mixtures, varying its prescriptions in some cases for a single genus of plants. Needless to say, this sort of sorcery has little to do with practical gardening.

Such things as sphagnum moss, pulverised tree bark, leafmould and charcoal, not to mention special drainage materials such as Cornish sand, all have a particular value, there is no doubt of it. Epiphytic succulents certainly seem to enjoy the inclusion of organic ingredients; and leafmould (sterilised) is a good thing to add to any compost, even to a mix which already contains peat. This playing about with mixtures can be great fun of course, but generally a standard mix will be suitable. It can always be modified for special purposes. If it should sound like a tall order to use one standard mixture for most of the plants to be grown, in practice it is not. Succulents, it should once again be noted, are very adaptable.

Whatever the type of compost chosen, it should be neutral with a pH of approximately 7; it should be porous, free-draining and loose to the touch. Some mixtures which seem quite suitable to begin with tend to cake or harden after a while, and this must be prevented. With plants which grow quickly the problem does not often occur, as they are usually potted on or re-potted fairly quickly. The plants to watch are the ones which grow slowly, the species which one does not expect to pot on very often. Succulents of this type can really be inhibited or even lose their roots if their compost settles down and packs hard, retaining too much water and excluding air. A good rule to follow is to try the density with a dibber. If it cannot be pushed easily into the mixture, the time has probably arrived for re-potting or potting-on. This little experiment should always be tried when it seems that a plant is not thriving as well as it should be.

One or two other factors can affect the condition of a compost. The prolonged use of hard water can bring about caking, and if lime (from the water) collects in the compost it can become like cement. Very hard water can be harmful to jungle succulents and epiphytes, which prefer an acid compost, although no succulents really like hard water. If the use of hard water is unavoidable, some of its harmful effect can be lessened if a small amount of Epsom salt (magnesium sulphate) is added.

Sometimes the plants themselves can bring about a deterioration in compost health. The natural urge of some species to settle themselves more deeply in their pots results in a compression of their compost, though this is not often serious. Much more so, if unnoticed, is the tendency of some others, once they have made reasonable root growth, to send out a carpet of fine roots at soil level or just below. In time, this layer of roots can become so dense as to resemble a typewriter mat. It will soon become quite impermeable to both air and water and often there is a sudden decline in the condition of what until then has been a healthy plant. The change in health may be indicated when an apparently happy specimen quite suddenly drops a number of its leaves.

The larger 'tree' crassulas, the *Crassula ovata* group, some of the large kalanchoes and similarly growing sorts are particularly prone to this condition which may be brought about by top watering. This is not necessarily bad gardening; but there are clear indications that it seems to encourage the formation of these root mats. Any water given, once such a mat has grown, will run off its edges, flow down the inside of the pot and then waste itself, unless the plant has also rooted into bench aggregate or is standing in a saucer. The grower has, he is sure, given the particular plant a good drink, whereas, in fact, the specimen may be absolutely dry.

The cure is simple, and it will not harm a strong growing succulent in the slightest degree. The mat of roots should be completely broken or cut away; there is not even a need to unpot the plant in most cases. Tip off the top dressing, cut away the root mat and replace it with fresh, loose compost, covering it with clean top dressing. Strong plants do not appear to suffer at all from such rough treatment and will soon regain their former health once they can breathe and drink again.

Newcomers to the growing of succulent plants, who have not yet decided upon a compost to use, may find the one in which most of my own plants have been grown for a number of years worth trying. This is a peat-based mixture, adopted originally because of the difficulty in obtaining good loam and leafmould. In practice, it has proved reliable and easy to mix. With slight modification it seems to suit all kinds of succulents, from desert types to rain-forest epiphytes. The base is sieved moss peat; to three or four parts of this is added one part of lime-free grit or sand and one of perlite. A small amount of dolomite magnesium is included, to correct the acidity of the moss peat (some of these peats are much more acid than others) and give the whole mixture a neutral character.

Composts of this type contain little or no nourishment, and this must be supplied by adding a powdered fertiliser, in the amount specified by its manufacturer. It is often advised that a fertiliser for cacti (and, by impli-cation, all other succulents) should be low in nitrogen content. The advice is not unreasonable; such formulae work well, especially for cacti and succulents of other families which produce little leafy growth. How-ever, there are many succulents which do make fast growth in their ac-tive season, much of it leafy, and which need to have this suitably fed. Caudiciform species are often a case in point. For these, just as for grass in a meadow, an occasional nitrogen boost can be a good thing. Moreover, it is undoubtedly true that all succulents, including cacti, will

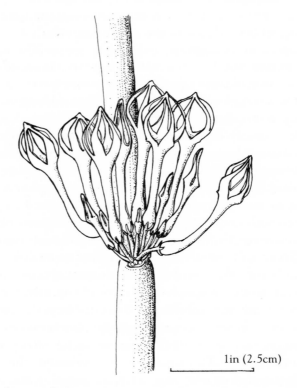

1in (2.5cm)

Ceropegia fusca belongs to the group which growers call 'stick' ceropegias. All are native to the Canary Islands, where they form thickets of erect or sprawling stems, usually in coastal areas. The flowers of C. *fusca* are reddish-brown, up to 1 1/2 in (4cm) in length, and are some-times borne in profusion.

benefit from one good feed of a nitrogen formula fertiliser at the beginning of their growing period. This is particularly useful if dormancy ends in early spring. During this season temperatures and bacterial activity are low. Probably, as with so many other things, variety has its value, and it will be most effective to use more than one type of feed.

Much more important than the amount of nitrogen present in a fertiliser is the number of trace elements which it includes. These additional substances are usually listed right at the bottom of the formula when this is given. Often a mixture will have only its main ingredients specified. Because trace element details are given this position in the list and are often printed in very small type, they are sometimes assumed to be of secondary, even minor, importance, particularly by the beginner. Nothing could be further from the truth. The lack of such things as magnesium, copper and, in particular, boron is a serious one. Only products which offer a full list of their ingredients should be trusted. The phrase 'with added trace elements' is not sufficient.

Most commercial composts, unless they are specifically prepared for succulent plants, will need the addition of extra drainage material. The amount must depend upon the compost in question but it is not critical. Experience and usage will soon show whether a mixture is draining freely enough or even too freely. There are growers who are successful with unmodified, manufactured composts. For species which are fast and strong growing they should be successful enough for many growers.

The arguments which flourish, nowadays, between the protagonists of what is called natural or organic gardening and their opponents, hardly have any place in the growing of succulent plants. Few of them seem bothered by such considerations. Nevertheless, our hobby does raise a special point of its own, an argument which is the reverse of the one usually raised in other branches of horticulture. The succulent plants which live in forested environments will receive natural nourishment from the humus-rich, organic soils about them. Droughtland species will be nourished by a mixture of soils but in cultivation they appear to show little preference. Desert succulents, on the other hand, will in most cases live upon inorganic deposits in the mineral-rich soils of these organically deficient areas. A need for what is called natural by the organic school must imply, in this specific case, what is natural in the desert, that is, inorganic feeding. It is certainly true that too much humus and organic nourishment in a compost has a tendency to produce lush, bloated growth in such succulents as the mesems and the slow growing, highly adapted desert cacti, which will grow, flower and look better in lean mix-tures which are composed principally of drainage materials and inert material such as vermiculite or perlite.

Pots and potting

Most flower pots used today are plastic, though some gardeners find them unattractive compared with clay pots, especially for favourite plants. There is little doubt that plastic pots will grow equally fine specimens, particularly in their smaller sizes. Very small clay pots, attractive as they may be, tend to dry out too quickly, even for desert plants. All in all, plastic containers seem to have most of the advantages. They are light, easy to clean, and they take up little space when stored. As well as these virtues they also offer the benefit of standardisation in size, weight and quality and good ones do not break readily . They are relatively cheap and they come in a wide range of shapes, sizes and colours, all of these things a great help to a gardener who is interested in showing off a collec-tion as well as possible.

Some clay pots are still being made commercially, but most of them are not what they once were. Like all clays made since the last war, they are machine-made and low-fired to save cost, and they soon break. If clays are wanted, better bargains can sometimes be picked up at country sales. These are the good old Victorian and Edwardian pots, still going strong and a few of them probably one hundred years old. They may be chipped but they date from a time when such products were high-fired in the kiln to toughen them. Clay pots were never easy to clean, particularly if hard water had left them with a deposit of lime, and stained with algae or moss. However, they can be brought back to a much better appearance if they are scrubbed with sand or rubbed over with an old red brick. Good pots deserve such attention.

Modern handmade clay pots can sometimes be obtained, plain, deco-rated, or glazed and finished in colour. Pots like these are often beautiful objects in their own right. They are not cheap, nor can one expect them to be; but any cultivator should consider them for choice plants. For showing they ought to be indispensable – it is always puzzling to see a large, probably costly specimen in a gaudy plastic washing-up bowl (nearly always a hideous red or yellow). Yet it happens all the time in Britain. Growers and exhibitors in other countries seem to have much more taste. Americans in particular frequently grow their plants in individual pots which have as much beauty as their contents.

Plastic pots, in spite of their overall value, possess one great disadvantage. They and their contents heat up very quickly in the sun and, if exposed to direct sunlight, do not have the ability to evaporate moisture through their walls. This was one of the virtues of porous clay pots, a process which kept them and their plants cooled to some extent. To prevent plastic pots overheating, either plunge the pots on the bench, or arrange them so that those which first catch the sun shade those behind them. A board fixed along the front or back of the bench (whichever faces south) will keep the heat off the exposed row.

The choice of pot size is really a matter of commonsense; it is not easy to be more specific. In general, select a pot which will hold the roots of the plant comfortably. This usually works although it can occasionally result in a specimen being given a container which looks too big for it, or a species with tiny roots looking as if it is bulging out of a tight suit. In either case, if appearance is important, a compromise is necessary. Bulgers may be given a large pot, which can have a deep layer of drainage material as its bottom layer. Tinies could have one or two easy seedlings planted round them, which would save space and encourage the seedlings to make better growth.

When considering the size of pot to use, do not be misled by those succulents (usually cacti) sometimes seen growing in pots which are obviously too small for them. In small collections, invariably kept by beginners, these are the victims of the wrong belief that succulents don't need to be re-potted – well, hardly ever. At specialist shows underpotting is an old exhibitor's trick. It allows a plant to be entered in a class where pot size is limited and gives the specimen more chance of a prize among smaller ones, unless the judge spots the attempt at deception.

Tree-like succulents, which make a sturdy central stem or trunk, can often be underplanted with small, shade loving species. Not only does this arrangement make the best use of space which would otherwise be unused, but it will often be found that the small plants do much better when given the chance to grow as they would in the wild. Succulents like the tall euphorbias which eventually make a tall, bare stem may even have slow growing climbers planted at their base, a practice which often results in a charming effect, most of all when the climbers open their flowers.

Some species of succulent, notably those belonging to the Liliaceae, have a habit of making long, thongy roots, as much as a foot (30cm) or

1in (2.5cm)

Crassula ovata, popularly known as the jade plant, comes from the Cape Province. In cultivation it will grow steadily into an imposing specimen, up to 3ft (1m) in height. Flowering is not uncommon and the small pink blooms, which appear during winter make an effective contrast with the shiny, green leaves and thick stem. Variegated forms are obtainable.

more long, even in young plants. These either find their way out through the drainage holes of the pot or content themselves with growing round inside its base, all the time forcing the plant itself up and out of the compost. On some occasions these roots will even climb up out of the compost, grow over the side of the pot and find a second, neighbouring pot, in which to try their luck. Roots of this sort may be cut hard back with impunity. If they are shortened to approximately the length of the plant's longest leaves (not quite so severely in the case of haworthias) it will take no harm. The cut ends of the root should be dipped into a liquid fungicide, or into flowers of sulphur (an old but good preparation). After drying for a day or so at most, re-potting can safely proceed.

Most succulents grow best, and are most protected from stem rot, if they are grown so that the bases of their bodies or stems rest upon the top surface of their compost, instead of being set into it, as is the usual gardening practice. Quick drainage and dry necks are what succulents need. The top of the compost should be covered with a deep layer of grit or small pebbles, leaving the usual space at the top of the pot for watering and tidiness. The grit layer should extend, roughly, from the base of the plant up as far as the growing mark, the useful 'Plimsoll line' which shows how much of the plant should show above its soil or top dressing. This line usually manifests itself as a change of shape, texture or colour, or even hardness, between the stem and root. Sometimes there is a marked difference in shape.

If there is no clear indication of the depth to which a plant should be potted, beginners will have to use their own judgement and learn from experience. At least a grit layer leaves room for error. Succulents, like certain other plants among which bulbs are notorious, seem to enjoy fidgeting up and down in their pots until they are quite comfortable. Some species pull themselves well down into their compost in wintertime to avoid cold; others do the same thing in summer to avoid water loss caused by excessive heat.

It is nearly always advised that such dwarf mesems as lithops, conophytums and fenestrarias should be planted as high as possible to prevent rotting. But, however good our own intentions, many of these species are not happy until they have set us right and pulled themselves deep down into their pots, so that nothing shows above the top-dressing. With succulents like these which are known to be extra-sensitive to rot it is always a good technique to set them so that the grit layer extends down below the depth of the plant body.

Top-dressing gives a much more attractive appearance to any pot plant and certain plants may have grit, pebbles or other material specially chosen to set them off. In the case of the 'mimicry' plants and some of the lovely, dark bodied South American terrestrial cacti, a top-dressing can be chosen to match the species and give a concealing miniature environment, similar to that which would surround them in nature.

If top-dressing is invaluable for helping to drain excess water from round the vulnerable necks of succulent plants, it will also help to keep the top of the actual compost cooler, make weed removal easier, and discourage moss, liverwort and algal growths. It also provides a cool environment, often shaded by the plant itself, where other small succulents may be grown and where chance seedlings may arise from self-sown seed in optimum conditions.

There is good sense in preferring to top-dress woodland and epiphytic plants with more suitable material, eg, peat, leafmould, tree bark, sphagnum or other moss. It certainly looks much more in character for plants of this sort, and drainage is not such a critical matter for them, although it should not be neglected. The only objection to these 'woodsy' materials for top-dressing is that they float away if one wants to water these plants by plunging them completely.

There are succulents, especially among the terrestrial cacti, which are shaped like a turnip or carrot, or like a spinning top. What looks like the plant is, in fact, the root. The 'plant', in gardening terms, is no more than the small top of the root. Such succulents need to be potted so that only this small top shows above the compost or top-dressing and this generally involves the use of a very deep pot. These can sometimes be bought and they are usually called 'Long Toms'. Plants which need them are as a rule very susceptible to rotting and it is safest to plant them so that an extra-deep grit layer surrounds the root, well down into the pot.

When these napiform (ie turnip-shaped) succulents are known to be difficult to grow they may be tried in pure grit or other drainage material. The pots can be stood on a grit or gravel bed, the drainage holes enlarged considerably, and all watering done from below with a dilute feed always added to the water. Using this method will encourage roots to grow below the pots and these may make considerable growth in their search for nourishment. Plant growth is not inhibited; if anything it is improved, and one can water well during the growing season, with less danger. A simpler method of growing succulents of this sort is to put several into one large, and therefore probably deeper, pot or pan.

Whether or not to use drainage material of some sort at the bottom of pots before filling them with compost is a matter of opinion. Some growers swear by it and others reject it completely. It used to be believed that a good layer of crocks or other drainage material below the compost helped it to drain more easily. However, recent experiments have shown, quite conclusively, that this is not so. The deeper the actual compost the better it will drain, if it is a good one in the first place.

Clay pots, or others which have large drainage holes, will have to have these covered, in order to prevent compost from trickling out when dry, or washing out during watering. All sorts of things were once used for this purpose; a piece or two of broken flower pot, small squares of perforated zinc, or even small cockle shells. Today, the simplest answer to the problem is to use a small square of plastic netting and cover it with a thin layer of coarse grit.

Re-potting

This word is usually taken to mean that the plant should have all, or nearly all, of its compost removed, its roots trimmed if necessary, and is then treated like a new acquisition. It should be given a new clean home, usually in a larger pot if growth has been sufficient for this to be necessary. For plants of the faster growing sort, re-potting may well be a regular annual requirement, although even with these potting on may be sufficient. Slow growing species may not need re-potting for several years.

The decision to re-pot or give a check-up depends upon several things. In the first place: is the plant thriving? If it is not, in spite of having all the necessary conditions for a healthy existence, check that a general loss of tone and colour is not merely due to a natural desire to go dormant, then knock the plant out of its pot and see what is wrong. It is never wise to let any plants, however well they appear to be, go on too long without at least a cursory inspection. Succulents are resistant plants and may not always show the effects of disease or insect attacks until these things are well advanced. Prevention is always better than trying to cure; it may be a cliché, but one to remember in gardening.

With some succulents an examination is not an easy thing to carry out. Very large, prickly cacti, euphorbias or agaves, for example, present obvious difficulties. Nevertheless, the attempt must be made. The plant itself should be examined closely, then the underneath of the pot and any roots which may be showing. In the case of very large pots, it may be possible, with or without help, to tip them over slightly and slide a hand mirror underneath, to make root inspection easier. Next, it is worth removing the top-dressing and disturbing the top inch or so of compost. Often these procedures will reveal the cause of a lack or loss of condition; one need go no further, but concentrate upon suitable treatment.

Of course there are times when caution is advisable. Succulents may hang fire after being re-potted, especially if their roots are hard at work out of sight. Plants from overseas may need to settle down after the stress of several weeks in transit. Beginners who are anxious to see new treasures actually 'doing something' often worry unnecessarily over their apparent reluctance to do so.

1in (2.5cm)

Kedrostis bainesii. These attractive, African, caudiciform, succulents have not been in cultivation for very long. Those species which are obtainable now, usually as seed, are not
difficult to grow and bring into bloom. Dry forest treatment is suitable, with the caudex raised
above the compost, to display it to its advantage.

Some succulents are capable of sitting out a whole season without making a move. Hoyas are notorious for this sort of behaviour as are species such as *Opuntia invicta* and *Euphorbia royleana*. Caudiciform succulents, too, can cause concern. Some species will, for no apparent reason, decide to go dormant at what (according to their previous habit) would seem to be the wrong time of the year. If they do, their wishes must be respected. It is also being realised that a number of succulents, some long in cultivation, are inhibited by long hot days, if the nights which succeed them are too short and do not cool sufficiently. (This applies to all countries distant from the Equator.) A good friend, who grows crassulas in Texas, has even resorted to using the refrigerator to overcome this problem with difficult species. Plants which behave in this way will make a good, even eager, beginning in spring, stop growing completely in midsummer and then start again when autumn approaches. (This problem is discussed elsewhere in this volume.)

With experience one learns to be suspicious of any new plant which comes into one's possession, wherever it comes from and however reliable the sender. Even plants from one's best friend should be very closely inspected before they are allowed to join the collection. Pests or diseases may not be present, but other, lesser troubles may well be. It is a pity that standards of potting are occasionally very poor. A drainage hole may be blocked or, in the case of plastic pots, not punched out properly during manufacture. Often the compost has not been mixed properly and contains lumps of clay, peat or stone, all of which may interfere with drainage and porosity of the medium. On one occasion I actually found a piece of glass, almost 1in (2.5cm) square, just below the surface of the compost. The plant was rare, a handsome gift for its recipient and it came from an amateur of considerable experience.

The most frequent potting fault lies in the depth at which plants are set. Even specimens set out for sale at commercial establishments may not be properly potted. Where they are tricky species they may have already been too long at risk to be worth buying. At the less scrupulous establishments one can also see imported cuttings which have few or no roots stuck deeply into pots of compost to hold them upright and then lined out on the sales benches. Here some slowly make roots and are all the time posing as properly rooted, growing plants. Beginners and the unwary are often caught by this trick. It is surprising how many purchasers do not bother to re-pot the plants which they buy. They assume that this is not necessary and, when their new acquisitions die, accept that this is due to their own lack of experience.

Pests may be present and even the best nurseries cannot be entirely trusted in this respect. Yet one must be sympathetic. There are some very resistant strains of some nuisances around nowadays and a grower or supplier may be forgiven for falling a little short of perfection. But it is only fair to let the seller know immediately if pests or diseases are found. If he is a scrupulous person he will be grateful for the information; if he is not, you will have been usefully warned. One should never believe anybody, whether amateur or professional who 'knows' that his plants are absolutely clean and healthy. He is either unobservant or a fool. At the same time, there can be no excuses made for the person who sends unclean plants through the post.

We are told, sometimes, that is is our present-day use of chemicals which has brought into being the newer strains of super-pests and diseases. Perhaps, after all, the Victorian way of dealing with these troubles was the most effective one – they destroyed any affected plant material, or even the whole plant, as soon as any pests or disease were seen. Or can

1in (2.5cm)

Echeveria lauii, one of the newer echeverias in collections; discovered in Oaxaca, Mexico, and not described until 1976. Among echeverias it is very highly prized by growers, but is not easy to grow well. Very good drainage is essential and moderate watering. The beautiful, white powdered leaves must not be wetted when water is given, as young ones will mark easily and those below may rot.

this be just another legend? It is far from easy to throw out any sick plant or cutting, let alone a rare, expensive one. One wonders if nineteenth-century growers were always as ruthless as it is said that they were.

Ideally, re-potting should be done just before the resting period ends to give a good start in the growing season, but, since this is not always practical, it can usually be carried out by any stage of the plant's growing cycle. It is certainly best to avoid the time when an individual specimen is in bud or flower. Many species will take this disturbance in their stride, but many of the epiphytic cacti will not do so and are rather prone to drop their buds if given a change while their flowering season lasts.

There are species which undergo a long rest period each year, during which time they are usually kept very dry, principally to avoid the accident of starting them into growth at the wrong time. The dwarf mesem group includes a number of such plants, the very highly adapted species, eg, lithops and conophytums being typical. These are best re-potted, if possible, approximately halfway through the dormant period, usually in midwinter. If the fresh compost is only barely moist it will give the plants just enough refreshment to prevent the fine roots from dying off, but not enough to start the plants growing.

Potting-on

Potting-on is a simpler process than re-potting and it takes less time. There is no disturbance of the plant and its soil ball at all. The top-dressing is tipped off, the plant is knocked very carefully out of its pot and any long roots which may have encircled the bottom of the pot are gently teased out, or cut back. A fresh pot, a size or two larger than the old one, should be taken and the plant set centrally into it. Possibly a little fresh compost will be needed at the bottom of the pot, as larger pots are usually deeper. Fresh compost should then be dribbled around the space between the soil ball and the sides of the pot, up to the level of the old compost. Top-dressing is added – and that is that.

Very large plants, which may be extremely heavy, and awkward to pot-on, do not need this sort of attention too frequently. However, there are succulent plants which grow extremely fast, if encouraged to do so, and these will respond to frequent potting-on by making a great deal of new growth. Several times in the course of a year is not too often when such plants are young and treatment of this sort can produce an imposing, background specimen of, for example, the larger kalanchoes, aeoniums, agaves and similar succulents. The beautiful tall growing kalanchoes in particular repay generous treatment and need it if they are not to become leggy and drop their lower leaves.

The after treatment of succulent plants which have been potted-on or re-potted should follow certain principles. In summer such plants should be stood out of direct sunlight, in shade or half shade, in a place where the air is not too hot or dry. In winter a brighter position is best, although extremes of heat, cold or damp should be avoided. Careful spraying may be of great assistance, particularly for specimens which have shrivelled during a long journey through the post. But great care must be taken to ensure that no surplus water remains in rosettes or in leaf axils or similar danger spots.

It is a good rule to rely upon the moisture of the fresh compost provided to support all plants which have been potted or re-potted rather than to water.

This also allows damaged roots or rootlets to recover more safely. Plants from overseas nurseries may have had their roots trimmed back to reduce weight, or even cut completely away to conform with regulations. In cases like this it is safest to dust the cut root ends with a powder fungicide and treat the new plant as a cutting and re-root it, preferably in a propagator. Importing plants from overseas nurseries is always a risky business, however conscientious the shippers may be, and a percentage of losses has to be expected. Succulent plants travel better than most other plants, but the time which it takes them to reach us, even with modern transportation methods, is still too long for some species. When at all possible, it is always much more satisfactory to buy seed of those plants required and grow one's own specimens. It is much cheaper, too.

•5•
Propagation

Most succulent plants are propagated from seed or cuttings and certain species lend themselves to layering or division. Grafting is a widely used technique in Europe and self-propagation is common if conditions are suitable. The more easily that succulents can be reproduced in cultivation, the better it will be for the species themselves and for everyone who has their interests at heart. It will also provide a way to combat the black market in imported wild plants.

Propagation has an effective part to play in conservation. Several parts of the world where succulents naturally make their homes are now under threat. The rain forests of Madagascar are fast disappearing, as are similar environments elsewhere, and even the desert areas and other wild places grow smaller as civilisation spreads ever outwards. It is a matter for regret that few of the commercial enterprises in this country (they can hardly be called nurseries) have given the attention to the propagation of rare plants which they might have done. The nurseries in North America deserve our praise and gratitude for keeping so many threatened species in constant supply.

Fortunately, there is a strong network of skilled and anxious amateurs around the world. Newcomers who develop special interests will not find it difficult to join a society which caters for them. There are a number of small organisations which operate their own seed distribution and exchanges and many members are also engaged in exchanging seed and cuttings with each other. All serious amateur growers should join and support at least one of these societies; their co-operation will help the plants which they care about, as well as increasing their own pleasure.

Seed-raising

Raising plants from seed is an absorbing and satisfying occupation which for many gardeners becomes the most rewarding part of their hobby. There is a real sense of achievement in possessing mature flowering specimens which began their lives as tiny, sometimes dust-like, seeds in the propagator. Few growers who take their activity seriously are content to continue buying adult specimens, unless these species are otherwise unobtainable. And if they then progress, as most do, to buying small seedlings to raise themselves, it is a small step on to buying seed and beginning to enjoy the whole of the process. There are also practical advantages to be considered in growing from seed. Seed is cheaper to buy than plants, even small ones, and it frequently offers the only way of obtaining those species which are no longer imported and which cannot be propagated from cuttings.

Among succulent plants there is much variation, even among the seedlings of an individual species. One small batch of tiny specimens may show an astonishing amount of diversity as they grow to adulthood. Not only can the basic shape vary, but there may be differences in the amount of hair, in the length and colour of spines, or in the rate of growth. There may also be variation in the flowers, when the seedlings are old enough to produce blooms, and it is this exciting attraction of the unknown which sometimes compels a grower to hang on to many more seedlings than there is really room for. One of them might produce flowers of a deeper colour, or even turn out to have the white blooms which are so desirable in species which are usually coloured.

Seed-raised plants are often better than those available from shops and nurseries. Commercial dealers have to sell all their stock; they cannot afford to throw away the specimens which fall below the standard of the best. The amateur, on the other hand, can afford to be much more selective. Any plant which is blemished, however slightly, can and should be scrapped, unless there are indisputable reasons for not doing so – usually its rarity and hence its value as a possible source of seed. Only the very best plants should be kept, as it is most important that the overall quality of plants in cultivation should be maintained, or even improved.

Some successful seed-raisers will tell beginners that the practice is easy; others try to present it as a deep mystery which is quite beyond the ability of lesser gardeners. The truth lies somewhere between these two extremes. Seed-raising undoubtedly needs skill; but it also needs commonsense and some of the qualities which a beginner may already possess. Technical facility will develop if the grower is able to contribute patience and exactness, has a tidy mind and is prepared to take pains in what he does. There is no reason at all why an intelligent amateur should not learn to raise most of his own plants from seed.

There are now several suppliers whose catalogues offer far more types of seed than any nursery could offer as plants. Most of the seed obtainable from all these sources is reliable, fresh, and has good viability. Nevertheless, there are occasional disappointments which have to be expected. Much of this seed is collected in the wild and it may be perfectly natural for a species, or even a whole genus of succulents to produce seed which has a low germination rate.

Ordinary horticultural seedsmen sometimes offer a small selection of succulent plant seeds and this often comes from the same sources which supply the specialist supplier, even if it is much more expensive. These commercial firms also make a practice of offering mixed seed and sometimes describe it as suitable for beginners. It should be avoided. One cannot always be sure that it is fresh or of top quality. If it is good, it may disappoint the novice more than if it were not. A good germination will bring its own problems, though it may seem to be an excellent way of beginning a collection if one raises a batch of different plants all at one go. It should be realised that, even if every seed in the selection germinated and began to grow well, it would be neither simple nor practical to give each of them the individual treatment which they might well need in order to survive. Even if the seedlings did survive, they would probably be impossible to identify and label.

It is best to use a propagator for raising seeds and for the novice it is almost essential. Only by using such a piece of equipment can one have proper control of light, fresh air, humidity and temperature. There are now a number of excellent propagators on the market. They are usually fitted with a built-in heater and thermostat and need only to be plugged into a source of electricity to be ready for use. Once a succulent plant collection is established, it will be surprising if seedlings of all sorts do not spring up of their own accord. This may seem to suggest that the exactness, attention to detail and, in fact, all of the basic recommendations for controlled seed-raising are really not necessary. The manner in which self-sown seeds behave may even suggest alternative methods of working. Nevertheless, it is wise to learn and to master a basic set of operations until sufficient command of them has been acquired. Only then will it be logical to think of varying them.

Next in importance to the seeds themselves comes the compost to be used. Fortunately succulent plant seeds, like the plants which they produce, are ready to accept a wide range of mixtures. Probably the simplest way of deciding which one to use is to keep to the standard mix which

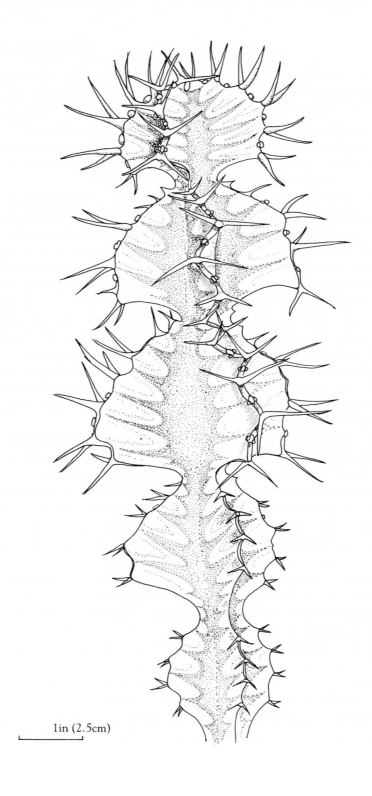

1in (2.5cm)

has already been found suitable for the plants in the collection. If it gives satisfactory results for these, it will probably be very suitable for seed-raising, with slight modifications.

First of all, the compost should be well sieved to remove any lumps or larger pieces of grit and give a more suitable mixture. Then a small percentage of fine grit should be added if the compost is on the coarse side, and the sieving repeated. The coarser sieving should be used to fill the seed pots or pans up to halfway with the finer part used above it to provide a good seed bed and encourage the growth of roots in the early stages. It is always a good plan to sterilise any compost especially for seed-raising. All grits should be well washed or boiled, and then screened before use.

Unless a large number of seeds is being sown, small plastic pots will be much more practical than seed pans. The average portion of seed is likely to consist of somewhere between ten and twenty seeds, that is, for the commoner species of cacti, mesems and similar species which have smaller seeds. Larger seeds, eg, those of some euphorbias, caudiciforms and stapeliads, tend to come in packets of five or less. Sometimes they are individually priced. If 2in (5cm) square pots are chosen (a most useful standard size and shape), each of them should comfortably hold one portion of seed, five or a few more opuntias or euphorbias and so on. In the case of very large seeds, one per pot should be sown. Before sowing seeds even new pots should be sterilised in a suitable liquid preparation.

It is important that each packet or species of seed should be given its own pot and should be correctly and fully labelled. Serious seed raisers are always buying or being given special seeds. Once information concerning its identity and source is separated from the seed itself, it may not be at all easy to put the two things back together again. All identification details must be entered on the label and also in a file index or other reference.

Enough room should be left above the surface of the fine top compost for a thin layer of grit to be added. Fine seeds should be scattered on this. Very fine seeds will be drawn down into the grit by capillary action once pots are watered; others will root through it and then pull themselves down or at least stabilise themselves. Large, round seeds like those of the

Euphorbia pseudocactus. In its native Natal this strikingly marked species makes dense bushes up to 3ft (1m) in height. As a pot plant it will remain smaller, but will be equally colourful, with rich green stems, usually marked in yellow, and bold red spines. This is an easy species, which will grow well if given droughtland treatment.

larger euphorbias and opuntias should be sown on top of the compost before the grit layer is added. Flat seeds, like those of the larger agaves and aloes, and seeds of stapeliads should be sown on edge or on end, pushed into the compost to their own depth, before the grit is added.

The advantage of using square pots is that it enables them to be fitted neatly into a large seed tray, in twelves or twenty-fours. If both pots and trays are bought from the same manufacturer this arrangement usually works out neatly. Trays with drainage holes are best and these can then be lined with thin sheet plastic cut to size. The reason for this apparently contrary procedure is a simple one. Should too much water remain under the pots after watering it is a far less awkward undertaking to get rid of it by pressing the plastic flat to the bottom at one corner, so that the surplus may drain easily away than to attempt the hazardous operation of tipping a tray which has no holes. Another sheet of plastic should be cut, just large enough to cover all the pots when they are placed together in position.

With seeds sown and their pots labelled and set in the tray, it is time to water, in fact to soak the compost, and at the same time to disinfect the seed and the compost. Cheshunt compound, Chinosol, potassium permanganate, or a similar preparation should be added to the water at the advised strength. The tiniest amount of washing-up liquid or wetting agent may also be added, to help the compost to take up the water. The solution should be poured carefully into the tray, thoroughly soaking the seeds without disturbing them. It will not matter if the pots remain standing in as much as 1in (2.5cm) of water since it is essential that the top surface of the compost remains moist until germination occurs. Then the trays should be drained.

Pots which germinate first may be placed in a duplicate tray in the propagator. Alternatively, the original tray may be propped up slightly at one end, and germinated pots moved to the higher and drier end.

It used to be thought that darkness was necessary if seeds were to germinate, but this is no longer believed. Plastic covers may be clear or translucent. The natural twenty-four hour cycle will provide a changing pattern of light and dark, and the stimulation which this affords is valuable. Further encouragement to germinate can be given by providing a change of temperature during each twenty-four hours. The temperature which is usually recommended for germinating succulent plant seeds is 70°F (21°C) and at this temperature very good success with many of the commoner species may be expected. However, it now appears likely that some species, perhaps those belonging to the Crassulaceae in particular, may be inhibited by a constant temperature. Tiny seedlings in the wild expect a nightly drop in temperature, even down to as low as freezing, and a corresponding rise by day. It is always safest to avoid extremes of any sort, but if a temperature range of say, 80°F (27°C) by day is alternated with a nightly low of 50°F (10°C) it is almost certain that better results will be obtained. More than once in my collection, surplus seeds of a particular species or type of succulent, scattered, as a rough experiment, on the plunge material of the greenhouse, have germinated faster and in better numbers than those cosseted in the propagator. Sometimes, germination has even occurred in an open position, with little moisture present, although this is exceptional.

After germination

Generally speaking, the seeds of succulent plants germinate quickly. Some members of the Asclepiadaceae may even show themselves in less than twenty-four hours, while others may take weeks or even months. Euphorbias can be very dilatory, as can some of the other Africans which have exceptionally large seeds. Typical of this group are the moringas and cyphostemmas.

After germination the seedlings should be given more light, to prevent etiolation. This means bright shade; hot sunlight may kill off, or burn, a promising batch of young plants. Water in plenty should still be given and this, if the seed compost does not contain any fertiliser, should have a small amount of feed added to it. Seedlings, it must be emphasised, should never dry out at any time. If the first soaking of the compost was made with a fungicidal solution, it would now be a good idea to complement this by watering the seedlings with a dilute insecticide, preferably a systemic. Tiny seedlings are very much at risk and must be given constant attention. All waterings during these early stages should be given from below, to prevent seedlings from being washed away.

Damping-off is a fungal infection which may attack succulent seedlings, although initial precautions should have prevented it. The problem is to prevent the fungi (*pythium* species and others) from appearing in the close conditions which are necessary for the seedlings, but which also favour the enemy. If damping-off is noticed a fungicidal watering should be given at once.

Moss or similar algal growths can be a bother at times. They are more likely to occur if a peat-based compost is used, but no mixture is absolutely immune. Vigorous seedlings, especially those of large species will usually cope with algae, but tiny, slow growers may be overcome by them. In most cases, the existence of these various green growths means that the light reaching the seedlings is too low in intensity. A change to much brighter conditions will usually cure the problem, unless the algae are already growing very strongly, in which case they may be able to adapt and persist.

There are two schools of thought concerning the after care of young seedlings. Both are successful – for some people. Few growers seem able to use both. One school believes in keeping seedlings tightly sealed away in their containers, sometimes for weeks or even months. The other school believes in the virtue of fresh air as soon as germination has taken place. Either the label is slightly raised, or a matchstick slipped under the plastic cover, to raise it. The fresh air method has the advantage of re-ducing the likelihood of a fungal attack and probably keeps down damping-off disease. It also makes it necessary to give more water, as moisture can evaporate more easily.

Whether one or the other of these two methods has more advantages must depend upon the individual raiser. Seedlings of all species but the very dwarf cacti and mesems should make constant, visible growth, which should not be checked. It is natural that more experienced grow-ers should be able to produce much larger plants in twelve months than beginners probably will. If the beginner can obtain the advice of a skilled cultivator, or be privileged to visit his collection, the experience should be invaluable.

1in (2.5cm)

Lithops species, the 'living stones' from South Africa – real desert plants, which grow and flower well if they are not spoiled by over generous treatment.

Pricking out

Pricking out is the process by which seedlings are transferred one by one from their seed pot or pan to rows in a larger one, so that they may have more room in which to grow and fresh compost to help them do so. The system has its critics and its champions and, once again, there are those on both sides who make their own methods work well., In theory, the benefits obtained from pricking out seedlings are obvious; in practice there are disadvantages. Seedlings so treated will inevitably suffer a set-back, however slight. Tiny roots will be lost or broken and will have to be grown again and during all this time the seedlings will be at a greater risk from pests or diseases. Yet once the convalescent period is over seedlings may begin to make better growth, although some species so resent root disturbance that they will sulk for months before starting to grow again. Fouquierias are probably the worst offenders, but they are not the only ones.

One answer to the problem is to leave seedlings to grow on in their seed pots; but many species will soon outgrow these and then grow no larger until something is done to help them. It is no answer to say that a thinner sowing would have helped; seedlings seem to like to grow fairly close to each other and in a clump will often do much better. Another advantage of encouraging them to do so is that once a clump is established, late-germinating individual seeds are more likely to survive down in the shelter of the earlier ones. The best solution, undoubtedly, is not to prick out seedlings one by one, but to pot on the whole clump as soon as it fills its pot, a process which can be repeated if necessary.

Pricking out seedlings can be a fiddly, exasperating business but potting on clumps of them is often much more difficult. Nevertheless, the value of the technique is so great that it should be learned, and the process will be made easier if the following method is employed. The new, larger pot should have a layer of fresh compost poured into it and firmed. A pot of the same size as the seedling pot can be placed into it as a 'mould' with its rim on the same level as that of the larger pot. More compost is then poured into the space between the two pots and firmed. If the smaller pot is then removed, the hole which is left should fit the clump of seedlings when it is knocked out of its own pot.

This process is not easy to describe, nor to carry out, and it needs skill and dexterity, if the soil ball is not to disintegrate. Much depends upon having a good rootball and making sure that the compost is not too wet.

However, seedlings so transplanted receive little check and the process may, with advantage, be used again for a second time if necessary. Once in its new pot and re-gritted, the seedling clump should show little sign of having been moved and can grow away contentedly. The method has one other advantage; it often seems to prompt a second germination which would almost certainly have been lost if the first batch of seedlings had been pricked out individually. Even a third germination is not unknown.

It may be argued that plants growing in this way, packed together in a clump, will not be as well-shaped as they might be if treated individually. In practice, however, once the clump has room to stretch, it does so. The seedlings push themselves away from each other, like a small expanding universe, to give themselves room for development. The few which may prove to be a little mis-shaped, when they are finally pricked out, will, as a rule, soon recover and be indistinguishable from their neighbours. There is, of course, no reason to prick out such natural clumpers as lithops and other mesems, or even some terrestrial cacti. Such plants always seem to grow and flower better, and look much more attractive, if not separated.

Whichever method is used for seedlings, after transplanting they should be rested for a few days without water in a cool, shady place. Then, when any broken roots have healed and the seedlings have settled themselves in they may be returned to the light. They will appreciate a light spraying and should quickly repay these small attentions with increased growth. This is the stage at which spiny succulents begin to develop strong spination if the light is good enough.

Opuntia basilaris, the Beavertail Cactus, forms low wide clumps, usually in desert-edge country, in company with sagebrush and scrub conifers. In cultivation it needs good light and room for its roots to spread out

•6•
Vegetative Reproduction

Vegetative reproduction is a term used to cover all those methods in which a part of one plant is taken and used to produce a new one. Such parts may be stems or pieces of stem, leaves or their buds, sections of roots, offsets, plantlets, suckers, rosettes or divisions. Tissue culture and micro-propagation are also possible in some cases, but are felt to be beyond the scope of this book. Succulents may often be reproduced in more than one of the above ways and, for those which do not set viable seed in cultivation, or which do not come true from seed, one of the above methods is the grower's only means of reproducing his own plants.

It is usually stated that plants propagated by vegetative means are identical to their parents, which is true if we mean genetically identical. In practice, though, it is possible for superficial differences to exist, both between parents and offspring and between the offspring themselves. To avoid this as far as possible only typical material should be selected for cuttings. This will reduce the chance of an unwanted variation in over-all appearance. (This precaution is not as necessary with succulents as it is when propagating some other plants. With dwarf conifers, for example, cuttings taken from different parts of the parent can produce plants of very different appearance.)

Succulent plants propagated from cuttings will usually give larger plants more quickly than those grown from seed, although this is not in-variably the case. Some cuttings are very slow to root and may even be outstripped by seedlings, if these are grown by a skilled propagator. What is true is that cuttings will usually produce plants already mature enough to flower in less time. This may be an important advantage.

Cotyledon orbiculata has many forms and a wide distribution in South Africa, especially in mountainous areas. The plant needs very good light to keep the leaves white and powdery. Quite young specimens produce impressive heads of orange bell-flowers

Although most succulent plant cuttings are co-operative and even eager to assist in their own rooting, experience will soon show which species can be dealt with more easily than others when optimum conditions are provided.

The propagating frame

Several factors are important for the successful rooting of all cuttings, whatever their type: temperature, the time of year, the plant's natural cycle, the level of humidity, the rooting medium and, most important of all, the suitability and vitality of the cutting itself. These various considerations will not be the same for all succulents, but, for practical purposes, a mean must be established. When a species of succulent will not propagate if given average conditions it obviously must be given special conditions. In general, the most sensible approach would be to provide something like the conditions favoured by the parent plant, modifying these to avoid excesses of any sort. Cuttings of desert plants will not accept great heat, nor those of epiphytes so much humidity.

It is almost essential to use a propagator for rooting cuttings. Experienced growers may not need one – at least not for easier subjects; but one can be fairly sure that they use one for more difficult things. It would not be practical to use a propagator for seed-raising and for rooting cuttings at the same time. A maintained temperature of 60°F-65°F (15°C-18°C) should suit general purposes, but, as with seed-raising, a cyclical approach which sets a higher temperature by day and a lower one by night may give better results. Whatever is decided upon, heat will be more effective if it is bottom heat, probably produced by a buried heating cable.

Many different substrates are successful for rooting cuttings. The best is still probably sharp sand, with or without the addition of sieved peat. Cuttings seem to be stimulated to produce roots more readily if a hard, irritant substance is used rather than a softer one. Whatever is chosen, it should be clean or sterilised, porous and quick draining. A fine material like soft builder's sand packs too closely together and any roots made in it will most likely die, either because they are too wet or dry, or because they cannot breathe.

The amount of moisture provided for cuttings should not be very great, although forest species may have more to encourage them than species from arid areas. Spraying is the best way to give moisture; a fine misting, whenever it is necessary, will provide the right conditions inside a propagating frame. Healthy cuttings will still have their own built-in source of humidity; what is added should be no more than is necessary to keep evaporation to a minimum. A tight frame will lose little of its humidity.

Whenever possible, cuttings should be taken from actively growing material. If, however, a specimen plant should suddenly succumb to rot during its dormant period, which is quite possible, especially if this coincides with our northern winter, the remains may well supply enough bits and pieces for cuttings. Dried properly, and with all unhealthy tissue cut away, it should be fairly easy for at least one or two of these cuttings to root in a warm propagator.

Before cuttings are put into a propagating box, they must have their cut surfaces dried and sealed by leaving them in a cool place, out of the sun's rays. In general, the ones that are easiest to grow will need no more than a few days, others a little longer. Experience will soon bring greater knowledge. A good rule is that the more difficult a succulent is to grow, the more difficult it will be to propagate, though this is not always so.

Some cuttings will be quite safe and soon root if they are set immediately into small pots of compost which is barely moist. Branches

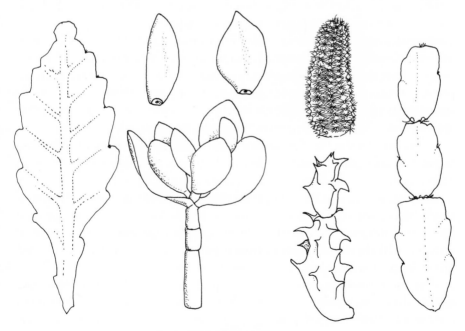

Typical succulent plant cuttings.

and pieces of stem of tree crassulas, sedums and kalanchoes, if large enough to grow in small pots when taken, might as well be rooted straight into them, if the usual precautions are taken. The cut surfaces should be dipped into a liquid or powder fungicide and then inserted into the pot. Rooting powders are hardly necessary for succulents; but any which contain a fungicidal ingredient, as some do, might as well be used for this benefit.

Cuttings from certain succulents are extremely susceptible to damp and must be given longer to dry, to make quite sure that the cut ends have calloused over and sealed themselves. Euphorbias are among the species which often take a long time to heal and it has usually been the practice to allow these to dry for as long as several weeks, to be sure that they are quite safe to go into the propagating frame. This precaution may be very necessary, but all the time that a cutting is forming a callus it is losing vitality and its stored moisture. When it is finally inserted it will stand far less of a chance to produce roots. Some propagators have, for this reason, been experimenting with alternative methods of dealing with the more difficult cuttings. One way, which has given good results, has been to stand the cutting, as soon as it has been dried and cleaned of its latex, into a solution of liquid fungicide, say for an hour, then to dry it off again and insert it straightway into dry sand.

My own experiments were carried out on different lines. An attempt was made to find a sealant which could be used on the cut end of a cutting, so that it could be set almost immediately into the frame when its vitality was at its highest. Various substances were tried. Nail varnish was effective, but expensive. Other trials produced what has given the best results so far – knotting. This is a mixture of shellac and spirit, used as a sealer in the decorating trade for the knots in new wood, before this is varnished or painted. The method of using it is simple and its value is high.

The cut end of a stem cutting is treated at once. It is wiped dry if it bleeds and then dipped into the pot of knotting, so that it receives a coating which extends ½-1in (2.5cm) from the cut end. As soon as the knotting dries and hardens the cutting is put into the frame. The coating of shellac keeps out damp (and possibly disease) and does not appear to inhibit the formation of roots or subsequent growth. As a rule roots will appear from just above where the shellac coating ends; but sometimes they will burst through it. Using this method has quite definitely given a larger number of takes in each batch of cuttings than older methods gave. More importantly, it has made it possible to root several species, not all euphorbias, which previously proved impossible or nearly so.

Euphorbias, like hoyas and some other asclepiads, have the property of producing a white latex when cut or damaged. This is poisonous and, in some species, extremely so. It has, in fact, been used by African tribes as a spear or arrow poison and extreme care must be taken when prop-agating any succulent plant which produces it. It might be safer to say 'when propagating all succulents' since many of the African succulents are new to cultivation, and most are quite unknown quantities as far as their possible toxicity is concerned. Euphorbia latex is sometimes very sticky and often succeeds in gumming up the edge of the tool being used to take cuttings. The help of a second person is invaluable. He or she can fill a small sprayer with very warm water, turn the nozzle to a fine jet and keep the cut sprayed whilst it is being made. Then, the job is quite easy, although large plants whose branches become woody may need to be severed with a pair of secateurs, or even a small saw, and then trimmed neatly afterwards. With small species of euphorbia it is often sufficient to dip the cutting edge of whatever tool is being used into surgical spirit, which breaks down the composition of the latex and removes it.

Leaf cuttings and stem cuttings

Many succulents will reproduce themselves from leaves, although the amateur who needs no more than one or two extra plants will find that they come much more quickly from larger cuttings – small side branches or even complete rosettes, if they are to be had. Nevertheless, leaf cut-tings will give good plants in time, if one is not in a hurry. They also have the advantage of not disfiguring the parent plant when they are re-moved.

Leaf cuttings must be taken with their growth buds intact, otherwise they will not be able to make new plants, though the lack of a bud may not prevent rooting. The bud, which is situated at the base of a leaf, against the stem of a plant, is easily damaged, more usually in the case of a succulent species which has thin leaves. Thicker leaves are easier to de-tach, by pulling them gently from side to side or giving them a little downward tug. When leaves do not come away easily it often helps to cut, very carefully, between stem and leaf, from each side, with a very sharp knife or razor blade. There are leaves which grow in pairs, with a central connecting section which clasps the stem. When it is possible to do so it is best to take a complete leaf pair and a short section of stem with it, but cutting above and below the leaves. If no more than one leaf can be spared from the parent plant, the knife should be used as before, removing a little surplus material from the centre of the leaf pair. This same method can be used for the species whose leaves are difficult to detach in one piece. A leaf can be taken with a section of stem remaining. The top of the stem will then make another good cutting and the fact of the stem itself being truncated may encourage it to branch.

Stem cuttings, when they can be spared from a plant, are essential for propagating succulent plants whose succulence does not extend to their leaves, or which do not possess them. The treatment for these is similar to that given to leaf cuttings. There are also succulents which must be propagated from stem cuttings or seed, even though their leaves are succulent. The leaves of such euphorbias as *E. decaryi,* and others will root easily but do not appear to form new plants readily, although some experienced growers have claimed reasonable success.

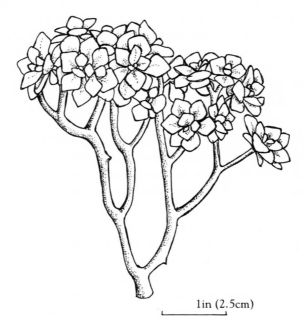

1in (2.5cm)

Aeonium lindleyi is one of the smaller Canary Island species, which lives in rocky areas. In cultivation it needs fairly spartan treatment to ensure that its dwarf habit and soft, green leaves do not become too lush.

Offsets and rosettes

In effect, a rosette is a very short stem cutting and should be treated as such. Many of them, and offsets too, will be rooted already when they are taken and so may be potted up straightway and grown on as young plants would be. A number of succulent species do not grow in an up-right manner, but make squat, stemless plants with smaller copies of themselves at the end of short branches. These may be detached, when they will usually root quickly in the propagator and grow away well. Left on the parent plant they will often root themselves down, or produce adventitious rootlets, so saving propagator space and the grower's time.

Cuttings from vining succulents may have different treatment. Many of them have a natural habit of producing adventitious roots at the nodes, or just below their leave bases, where leaves are present. If sufficient plant material is available, it is a good idea to take a long section of stem, cut off and discard the thinner end (which will probably wither anyway) and then lay this stem flat in a tray of rooting medium and press it down firmly. Once good rooting at the nodes is seen, the cutting need not be taken up. Instead, each rooted section can be separated from its neighbour by cutting through the stem at this point and dusting the freshly cut ends with a powder fungicide. Frequently, each rooted section will soon make a growing point which will produce a stem of its own. Potting up need not be carried out until the new plants are growing strongly.

Similar treatment will help to propagate climbing cacti such as selenicereus and their like. They do not, of course, possess nodes, but will root along the length of short sections of stem, if these are laid flat instead of being inserted vertically into the rooting medium.

Terrestrial cacti of the sort which have jointed stems (opuntias are typical) will also root more quickly and reliably if given the same propagation. Many of them grow naturally by extending new growth outwards rather than upwards. Chains of new pads will grow in all directions rooting as they go, until a sizeable patch of ground is colonised, a way of increasing which is common among the dwarf species and which offers an easy way of proceeding. Specimens of plants cultivated in this way in shallow pots or seed pans invariably have joints ready rooted and available for detaching and potting-up at once.

Cuttings should not be inserted too deeply into the rooting medium. Most require only to be laid or stood upon it, or pushed into it as they need to be to stand upright. Species known to be easy prey to rot may be stood round the sides of a small pot which has an inch or so of medium at its bottom (in the propagator). Leaf cuttings should be slightly inserted upon their budding bases, in an upright position. It is, incidentally, normal for the leaf itself to die away once a bud and roots begin to grow and nourish themselves upon the leaf's substance.

Impatience is an understandable failing and even old hands at propagation have been known to lift cuttings to see how they are getting on. For the most part this is unnecessary and may be harmful to progress. It is very easy to damage root tips or even break tiny roots away. In the case of cuttings which are very prone to rot there is a little excuse for a grower's anxiety. Such cuttings should not have their bases inserted into the substrate in the first place. Rooting should be indicated by a cutting making new growth, or perhaps by recovering from its stressful condition and taking on a healthier glow. But, even at this stage, patience should be used; better to leave all cuttings for a while longer, although they may be encouraged to grow if a little very dilute feed is poured over their bases. The moment will soon arrive when it is obviously time to lift the cuttings and pot them up.

As to the best time of year to take cuttings, there is no single recommendation. They are most viable when they are taken from actively growing plants, whenever this may be. If this happens to be a time of great heat, cuttings from some species may root in a very short time indeed, whilst others sulk until it is cooler. Almost any time of year seems to suit easier, commoner succulents; they will even root without the need of a propagator in wintertime. The commercial grower in any branch of horticulture must often taken his cuttings when he has time to do so. Obviously, his greater skill gives him the advantage but it also points to the need for some flexibility in one's approach to the business of propagation.

Grafting

Grafting is a method of effecting a union between the parts of two separate plants so that a new one is produced. Except for one or two techniques used principally for fruit trees, grafting consists of taking a rootless piece of one plant (called the scion) and uniting it with the root system of a more vigorous or free-flowering one (called the stock), in order that it may benefit from this stronger growth.

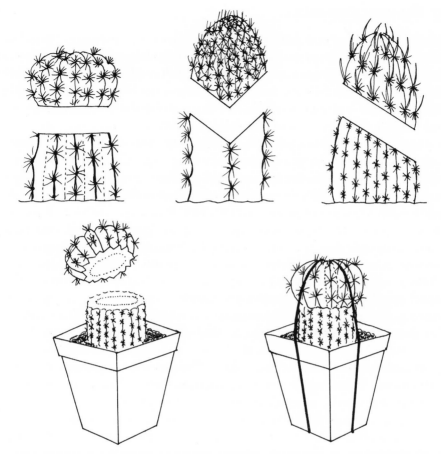

Common method of grafting. It is important to see that the cut surfaces of both scion and stock are more or less equal in area, so that the vascular bundles coincide when the two pieces are put together.

Among succulents grafting is usually reserved for cacti and is used mostly in such countries as Germany and Japan, where there is a large commercial trade in these plants. Grafting allows the mass production of large numbers of plants, which can be cultivated in one standard way and which will, in a short time, reach a standard size and possess a standard appearance. (A similar situation exists in the rose growing industry.) As far as the private grower is concerned, his cacti will probably do as well on their own roots as on those of anything else. There are plenty of examples of species which were once thought to be impossible to keep alive unless on grafts, and which are now not even regarded as difficult to grow and flower on their own roots.

Slow growing cacti, such as ariocarpus species or aztekiums, stand a much better chance of surviving their tricky, early days if they can be grafted as tiny seedlings on to stock of trichocereus or pereskiopsis (or equally useful, vigorous species), and a similar reason is now persuading raisers of other succulent families to make use of grafting. But apart from exceptions of this sort, grafting is best reserved for accidents and the technique should be learned; it may sometimes save a valued specimen, or at least enough of it to matter.

The basic technique for grafting cacti consists of preparing a stock by cutting its top off and bevelling the edges of the stump, to prevent the soft centre from shrinking down into a hollow. The scion is cut just above its base and the two parts to be united are brought together, so that the vascular bundles coincide, and are held together until they grow as one. The process should be carried out quickly, before the two cut surfaces dry, and various means are used to hold the two plant pieces together. A weak rubber band may be passed below the pot and stretched over the tip of the scion. Sellotape, or a similar product, may be used in the same way, or an adhesive sealer may be painted over the join.

Whatever the graft it is essential that both stock and scion should have a fairly close relationship; a cactus and a euphorbia are not likely to grow together. Very slow growing or tricky euphorbias should benefit

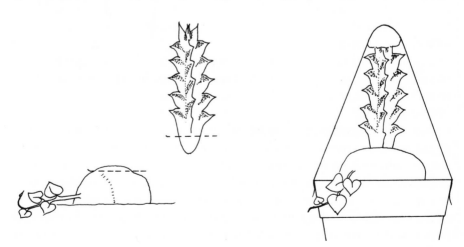

Asclepiad species, which are often attacked by rot at the base, may frequently be saved if the damaged stems are cut back to clean growth and then drafted on to a ceropegia tuber, as shown here. If a supply of tubers is grown specially for grafting stocks, they may be grown on their sides (as in the illustration) which facilitates the removal of the necessary slice.

from being grafted on to tougher, easier species, and the tubers of *Ceropegia woodii* and similar species will often be useful for more difficult asclepiads. Grafting is also being increasingly employed for other succulent plant families and genera, notably pachypodiums.

Grafting has one or two other uses worth noting. Crests and monstrose forms, which are very popular with some growers, will often not grow on their own roots and neither will plants which do not have their own supply of chlorophyll (the red and yellow cactus forms, imported and usually sold in supermarkets are a case of the latter condition). Certain cactus stocks are sometimes held to be of use for increasing the flowering propensities of this species or that; but the belief may have no foundation – proper methods of cultivation are probably just as effective.

Other considerations

The advice offered in this section may be seen as a counsel of perfection. It should be. It will not be long before any observant grower begins to devise successful alternative methods of propagation. There is, after all, never one way only of solving any problem. Most of the species belonging to that huge family, the Crassulaceae, need very little special attention. Not only do self-sown seedlings of the crassulas, sedums, kalanchoes, dudleyas and others spring up among the pots on the bench, but nearly every leaf which is knocked off, or any piece of broken stem which falls from a specimen which gets too dry, may well root itself and grow into a new specimen. It is often not only curious but downright frustrating to see a fine, new specimen suddenly show itself on the bench, which looks better, grows better, colours up more vividly and then flowers more abundantly than the cossetted specimens around it. The last straw is to find that this foundling is rooted, but barely so, into a thin layer of nothing but grit and supported against the nearest pot, and apparently nourished solely on what happens to leach out of the nearby containers. It goes to show that our plants are determined to survive – somehow.

Experience will show that few of the easier succulents, and a number of those which are considered more difficult, really need the bother and expense of propagator treatment. Leaves of many echeverias, for example, may be detached and simply stuck into the top-dressing under the shade of the parent plant. Small stem cuttings of suitable, easy subjects will root if treated in the same way. If space is used economically, few large plants should have bare space surrounding their trunks, at least on their shady sides; such places will root dozens of odd bits and pieces in the course of one year. Propagator space should be reserved for subjects which need it and which ought to have close attention.

It is always worth trying what may seem to be a 'wrong' method of increasing one's plants. The advice given in many books is sometimes too dogmatic and exclusive. For example, most specimens of the rare and popular *Ceropegia conrathii* have been imported and seed is not often available. The large tuber of this species, in common with other members of the genus, does produce new tubers on top of the old one (which is nearly always grown above ground in cultivation). These smaller tubers will make satisfactory plants if potted-up, but few are produced. Alternative methods of propagating this very lovely caudiciform are seldom, if ever, suggested. Yet every one of the short perennial stems on which the flowers are displayed will root quite quickly in a warm propagator and soon produce its own tuber. There is, therefore, no reason why this scarce and desirable ceropegia should not be available cheaply and in quantity. It is always worth trying similar experiments with caudiciform species. Very often it will be found that their vining growth will root and form new plants. Indications of some possibilities are given in the second part of this book.

•7•
Pests and Diseases

Luckily, succulent plants are not subject to many troubles, although there are one or two which are very persistent. Care and attention are needed at all times, and as with other forms of gardening it is much more satisfactory, and far easier, to cope with pests and diseases in the early stages of an attack than to let them get a good foothold before they are noticed. The problem that we face with succulents is that so many of them seem almost as if they were designed to provide cosy little retreats for tiny enemies. Some of the latter are difficult enough to see even when they are not hidden under spines, hair or wool, or tucked away down among roots. It is an easy matter for these nuisances to settle into their chosen hide-outs and multiply before they are suspected. Only a very short time is needed for some sort of infestation to take hold and inflict a great deal of damage. For this reason, attention must be constant.

A routine of spraying or dipping and close inspection of all plants should be established. It is most important that the chemicals and other remedies used should be varied, to give them the best chance of being effective.

There are now strains of pests and forms of disease in existence which seem almost to thrive upon some of the newer fungicides and insecticides. This is not to suggest that these should not be used, but rather to point out that some of the old, simple remedies can still be very effecive. A combination of both sorts will prove to be the most satisfactory way of coping with all troubles which may arise.

So called 'natural' methods of fighting diseases and pests are now much in vogue in some quarters, and it would be a blessing (and much less expensive) if they could be used in the proper management of succulent plants. Most horticultural chemicals are poisons and their toxicity, especially that of some of those used in modern preparations, can be as harmful to the grower as to the chosen target. On the other hand, the natural methods, which involve such techniques as the breeding and employment of predator insects, are not of much practical value, however much one would prefer to use them. The word 'practical' must be stressed; while theories are being tested or some of these suggested methods put into operation, plants can easily die or at least be irreparably damaged or disfigured.

Good, economical and practical methods of solving the problems of pests and diseases without recourse to possibly harmful chemical preparations would be a boon for succulent plant growers, as some have already proved to be for other gardeners. Anybody with time, patience and imagination is urged to experiment and pass on his successful results to the rest of us, as some growers are in fact doing. The problem in our greenhouses is that nearly all of us grow very mixed collections of succulent plants, which have many different needs even when perfectly healthy. A single horticultural crop which is grown and harvested uniformly can have its greenhouse emptied for attention. Our methods of management are, of necessity, more complex.

We can take a tip from commercial greenhouse growers however and empty our greenhouses completely, once a year. For the collector who has only a small greenhouse, such an undertaking may not be too arduous a task. The enthusiast who has a large house might find it possible to empty part of it and then hang up a sheet of plastic, so that the rest of the collection is effectively isolated and protected, while re-painting, fumigation and thorough cleaning are carried out. Such an annual chore will do more to reduce the likelihood of pests or disease than any other single endeavour. As for the plants which are removed, they can be safely stood outside in the garden (only a hailstorm would be likely to damage them) if the weather is reasonably warm. As each one of them is put back into the greenhouse, after sufficient time has been allowed for paint or preservatives to dry and fumes to dissipate, it can be thoroughly inspected and, if necessary, treated or re-potted.

Pests

Most of the pests which attack succulent plants do so by sucking the sap from within the plant cells. Those most likely to be a problem are mealy bug, root mealy bug, red spider and, occasionally, scale insects. Regular use of systemic insecticides will do a great deal to keep these and other insect pests in check; but, as already mentioned, there are indications that resistant strains of some insects, particularly of mealy bug, are now in existence. Even so, both systemic fungicides and systemic insecticides are now so freely available and easy to use that they will provide a fairly reliable general treatment for all succulents, to which may be added remedies suitable for dealing with specific ailments if these should occur.

Mealy bugs

There are two kinds, both of which show themselves as tufts of white substance rather like cotton-wool, in which the bugs hide themselves and breed. Above ground one will find those mealy bugs which attack the stems or leaves of plants frequently hiding themselves in leaf axils and other places which help to conceal them. Root mealy bugs, in contrast, are to be found on the surface of the compost, or just below it. Their choice, as the name makes clear, is for the roots of succulents, and they are obviously not so easy to spot.

Given that routine watering with systemic insecticide is carried out, it is advisable to supplement this by an occasional spray with a contact insecticide, such as malathion or one of the more 'natural' chemicals, derris or pyrethrum for example. A useful remedy for spot treatment, when the odd bug is noticed, is methylated spirit, which has a small amount of nicotine dissolved in it (a clean cigarette end may be used). This mixture can be used on a small watercolour brush and will be most effective. Nicotine or nico-soap solutions are also effective for contact spraying and soaking, if they can be obtained.

Red spider

This is a small reddish-brown mite, scarcely visible to the naked eye. It is not a spider, but was so called becase it spins fine webs. The presence of this troublesome pest will be shown very clearly as a yellowish or brownish discoloration on the plant body, most frequently at the growing point, where young growth is softer and less resistant. The methods advised for the treatment of mealy bugs will be equally useful for dealing with red spider, a pest which thrives best in dry, airless conditions. Plenty of fresh air will help to keep it away.

If what looks like an attack of red spider is noticed, the damaged plant should first of all be examined closely, if necessary with a hand lens. A very similar effect, on the growing point of a plant body or stem can be produced by trace element deficiency (see the section on Diseases).

Other pests

If the pests already discussed can be overcome, or at least kept to a minimum, most of the succulent plant grower's problems will be over. However, there are minor troubles which sometimes occur; if they do, and if they are of insect origin, they should be tackled along the lines suggested above.

Greenhouses always seem to attract various nuisances, particularly as the year dies and it offers a warm haven. Creatures such as frogs and toads, snails and slugs, or even mice will soon be discovered by the attentive gardener and removed. Frogs and toads certainly help to keep the insect population down and seem fairly immune to the small amounts of spray drift which must reach them from time to time.

Woodlice are popularly supposed to eat only decaying or decayed material; but this is far from the truth. They can and will eat green plant stuff and can do quite a lot of damage, especially to tiny seedlings. One of the poison baits, sprinkled between pots, or under them will be effective against these and other creatures of the crawling sort.

If it is the gardener's intention to leave the greenhouse door open at times it is wise to fit a board across its base, to keep out intruders. Snails, which always make for the choicest plants, will get in somehow, whatever one does to exclude them. Once again, a poisonous bait is the answer; luckily the snails seem to prefer it to plant stems or leaves once it is put down.

Diseases

As a group succulents are virile and resistant, though they can succumb to the usual pests and diseases. If looked after properly they will give little trouble, and when kept with other greenhouse plants, it is the succulents which are usually the healthiest.

The greatest problem is that of rot, and it is usually taken for granted that this is caused by giving a succulent plant too much water. However, this is often the old 'desert plant' myth at work again. Of course one can give too much water; but this statement must be qualified. A succulent plant which is a fast-growing species enjoying its growing period can hardly have too much water and nourishment, while the same amount, or even half the amount would certainly cause it to rot during the dormant period.

Cheiridopsis peculiaris is a member of a very large genus, spread over dry regions on the west side of South Africa. In the greenhouse, flowers of the Cheiridopsis species will do much to brighten the late winter months

Again, a compost which has lost its porosity, for some reason or other will hold too much water throughout its bulk, and roots compressed within will deteriorate and be unable to breathe, let alone take up water. The rot which will soon set in must, in this case, be blamed not on the amount of water given, but on the poor nature of the soil mixture.

Rot can also set in if an attack of root mealy bug begins and is not discovered in time, a reminder that one's attention has not been as regularly given as it should have been. This trouble is particularly prevalent among the stapeliad group, those African succulents with the lovely, if sometimes evil-smelling carrion flowers. Rot is, in fact, the one thing which spoils the growing of these fascinating plants and it even affects the collections of skilled specialists. As it happens, rot is also an affliction of stapeliads in the wild. Whole areas have sometimes had their stapeliad populations decimated when the climate has unexpectedly been too generous with its rain.

Deficiency diseases
In recent years it has been discovered that the ill effects of trace-element deficiency can be as harmful to succulent plants as to other members of the vegetable kingdom. The fact that this state of affairs was not recognised earlier is probably due to the old notion that succulents needed little water and less food. Time and time again one comes across the recommendation in older books that fertilisers should not be used, when in fact desert soils are usually very rich in minerals and jungles are a rich source of nourishing humus.

There can be few plants in our collections which do not need to be fed when they are growing, and it must be remembered that the food which we give them can be used only if it is in compost which is at the very least moist.

Some of the artificial feeds now obtainable have only the principal ingredients listed, plus the information that the mixture includes trace elements, but this is not enough. Purchase only those products which are

Argyroderma roseum. The 'silver skins' are dwarf mimicry plants from the western Cape Province. They are not difficult to grow or to raise from seed, but must not be over-watered, for fear of the bodies splitting

Crassula pyramidalis grows as a low, branched plant in the drier areas of the southwestern Cape, where there is winter rain. Mature branches produce attractive scented flowers, but die after ripening their seed

labelled with a complete analysis, and check that they have all essential ingredients, especially boron.

Information on boron deficiency is not always easy to come by. Even the work which has been carried out on agricultural and other commercial plants is of recent date, and experiments with succulent plants have mostly been made by observant amateurs. Nevertheless, it has quite definitely been established that, even if other more commonly known trace elements are present, the absence of boron will inhibit the proper growth of all plants, while its inclusion in a fertiliser seems to be essential for the healthy development of roots and meristems (growth points).

As noted in the previous section, there is a superficial resemblance between the damage caused by red spider and that caused by boron deficiency. A hand lens will soon show if the trouble is caused by insects. However, until recently, it was all too often assumed that any corky, brown disfigurement not resulting from scorching, had to be a red spider attack, especially if the damage was seen on young tender growth. Boron deficiency was not understood and therefore not suspected.

The result of dosing a succulent suspected of suffering from boron deficiency can be quite dramatic. The amount of boron must be carefully controlled. The substance may easily be obtained from any good chemist in the form of borax, a white powder which is not poisonous and which is easily dissolved in water. 1.7gm (only) of borax dissolved in 1 litre of water and 1cc (only) of the stock solution should be added to 1 litre of water again. Even at this rate of dilution the results of one or two doses on one plant may be seen surprisingly quickly.

•8•
Succulent Groups

It must be stressed that the groups of plants given special attention in this chapter are gardening groups. The succulents in them are placed together not because of botanical similarities (although these may be present) but because they share cultivational needs when grown in artificial conditions. Once the wishes of the plants in each of these groups are properly understood, it should be much easier to grow and flower them, even if it is in the nature of things that some will be more difficult than others.

The list of plants that follows gives more detail for the treatment of some particular species, where necessary. It should be born in mind, however, that for gardening purposes the most important thing to know about any plant is what sort of plant it is, in this case which group it should be associated with.

Euphorbia, for example, tells us only that a specimen has been placed by botanists into a specific genus. All the species in that genus share certain floral characteristics; they may come from widely differing habitats and be adapted to a number of quite different patterns of weather, climate and so on. If we are given plants which are properly labelled *Euphorbia supernans, Euphorbia lophogona, Euphorbia canariensis, Euphorbia ingens* and *Euphorbia namaquensis* and attempt to grow them all in the same way, just because each one is a euphorbia, we shall be lucky to keep them all alive for very long. Gardening and botany are quite different subjects.

Droughtland succulents

These may, for practical purposes only, be regarded as the 'norm', although there is really no such thing in such a large and varied group as succulent plants. Perhaps it would be better to say that the methods outlined in this section will suit most of the succulents to be found in the majority of collections. It is also true to say that these are the species which the beginner is most likely to come across in his earlier days. The notion which may arise from these considerations, that they are beginners' plants, should not put more advanced growers off growing them, nor should it give newcomers to our hobby a sense of inferiority. Droughtland succulents are probably the most colourful and certainly the most varied group of all.

The treatment for droughtland plants should, in general, incorporate the following points. All sorts should be given as much air and light as possible, at all times of the year. They must, however, be protected from too much direct, concentrated sunlight, particularly in unventilated conditions, and should not be exposed to cold draughts. When the cold time of year makes it essential to keep the greenhouse closed, a good fan will do much to keep the enclosed air healthy and buoyant, and rid the atmosphere of the damp, stagnant conditions which may otherwise occur.

All succulent plants should be allowed a rise and fall in temperature during each twenty-four hours. Warm days and cool nights are both necessary for a succulent's well-being and only if they are both experienced is a plant able to carry out the physiological processes natural to it. To simplify a very complicated process, it is only necessary to know, for practical gardening reasons, that succulents have a different respiratory cycle from that experienced by non-succulents (mesophytes). Succulents keep their stomata (the breathing pores) closed by day, and open them only at night when conditions are cooler and darker. In this way necessary gas exchanges may be carried out, and transpiration (the loss of vitally necessary moisture) is kept to a minimum.

As most succulent plants are natives of the more equatorial areas of the world, they are not naturally adapted to the long or short nights of the north (or south). It has been realised in recent years that many succulents may be as inhibited by our short, warm, summer nights as they undoubtedly are by our winter conditions. The British Isles are spared the hot summer nights experienced in parts of the United states, where I know of two collectors (one in San Francisco and one in Houston) who have put specially valuable plants into the domestic refrigerator each night during hot spells. Indeed, the Houston enthusiast has been compelled to give up a number of his plants which simply do not thrive in the Texas summer.

Droughtland succulents are much hardier than used to be thought. Many of them originate in places where frost, and even snow and ice, are not unknown. In cultivation they do not seem at all bothered by an occasional steep drop in temperature at night, even down to freezing or lower. But it is important that we as gardeners do not subject our plants to the most extreme conditions. We should do our best to iron out the greatest differences in temperature which naturally occur wherever we may live. Ventilation and shade will prevent the thermometer rising too high during the day; try not to let it register above 85°F–90°F (30°C–32°C) for droughtland plants. Sufficient heating should be installed to keep the night-time temperature from falling below 40°F (5°C), which should suit a general collection of succulents in this group very well, although some will stand a lower temperature quite safely.

1in (2.5cm)

Huernia stapelioides, showing twin seed cases called follicles which eventually split lengthwise, to release the seed. Each seed has a 'parachute' of hairs and is carried away from the parent plant by the slightest breeze.

Observant succulent plant growers are beginning to believe that many of their plants, of all types, might excel if given artificial light and heat when winter days do not provide these, and minimal heat at night. In this way natural conditions would be more closely followed. This method of cultivation makes very good sense; but much more practical experience of growing a great variety of plants needs to be gained before firm rules can be laid down.

One further point should be made. It has long been believed that all succulent plants are better for being allowed to dry right out during their rest periods. Succulents, it has been argued, are safest at very low temperatures only if kept absolutely dry. Those losses which have occurred in

1in (2.5cm)

Gasteria maculata, an attractively marked species found in several forms and widely distributed in South Africa. Gasterias will grow well in less light than most other succulents, although too much shade will cause the leaves to lose their distinctive markings. These are very good plants for indoor growing.

these conditions have usually been blamed on the cold, or the fact that casualties were not as dry as they should have been, or on some other mysterious reason. However, there has recently been a change of thought in some quarters; perhaps a slightly moist condition for a plant's roots will keep it in a healthier state and help it to cope with extreme cold. Complete dryness allows fine roots to die back and this means that they must be grown again before the plant itself can make much progress when a new season demands it. Most droughtland plants in cultivation seem to be better without too long and too dry a resting period, even when this occurs in winter. Nevertheless, it is important not to give so much water during really cold weather and when plants are dormant.

It may be argued that succulent plants in their natural habitat, do not receive such studied attention, and that they may sometimes go without rain for a year or more. This is perfectly true. However, plants in their natural homes are able to push out taproots or fine, feeding roots far beyond the confines of a small pot. They are therefore able to make use of each tiny drop of dew or mist which may still reach them. They are frequently found growing in rock fissures or similarly advantageous positions, where any precipitation, however small, can collect. Again, it must be remembered that some succulent plants in the wild do not survive their dry periods. They live on only through the new generation of seedlings which is born when rain eventually falls again. This, incidentally, is certainly one of the reasons for succulent plant seeds being endowed with such long term viability.

Desert succulents

As already explained, very few of the succulent plants in cultivation are from real deserts, therefore 'desert' treatment should be reserved for a few of the most highly adapted species. Such succulents as astekiums, ariocarpus and copiapoas will qualify, as will those more highly adapted South African succulents, such as the dwarf mesems, the dwarf crassulas, a few pelargonium species, some euphorbias and the like. In general, treatment for all of these succulents should be similar to that given to the droughtland group, but extra care should be taken and there will always be a danger of over-watering.

Desert soils are often poor in humus, but they are rich in minerals, so desert succulents are well fed once their soil is moistened by rain, mist or dew. Some growers prefer to grow trickier plants of this type in a compost made up entirely of grit, sand or other drainage material, and supply nutriment as a dilute feed at each watering. When actively growing, these desert plants welcome generous watering and spraying. In the wild they may well achieve a bloated, oversized and lush look which would get them disqualified by any judge at a horticultural show. Nevertheless, this growth will often get them through the dry periods which have to be endured. In cultivation even these desert succulents should not be allowed to dry out completely, for the reasons already given.

The position chosen for plants of this group should always be the lightest possible, to keep growth typical and compact. Many of them will be growing and flowering during winter and at this difficult time of year every effort should be made to brighten the dull, northern days, and to warm them as well. It is well worth installing fluorescent lamps, if one

1in (2.5cm)

Aeonium nobile, found principally in the Canary Islands. It grows as a stout-stemmed plant with a rosette up to more than 18in (45cm) in diameter. The inflorescence is a large one and the flowers coppery red. All aeoniums are natives of the Mediterranean area.

wants to grow desert plants well, and to fix them so that they can be lowered quite close to the plants themselves. The low heat from fluorescent lamps will not harm specimens, but will in fact be of benefit. Cold nights present no problems. Even a touch of frost will probably not damage most plants and some of them will not be harmed if the temperature drops even lower. Nevertheless, it would be a practical method of growing these succulents to plunge their pots into a bed of sand, warmed during the day by an undersoil cable. This could be switched off at nightfall, when the bed would act as an efficient storage heater, slowly releasing its warmth. In a severely cold spell, of course, the cable could be left on at night.

Desert succulents have several advantages for the collector who has a small greenhouse and who cannot afford to spend a great deal on heating. Most plants in this group are small and slow growing, as one would expect them to be. They are also tough and require minimal heating, and a collection could be made which would give interest and flowers all the year round. One more important advantage should be added. Most desert succulent species can be obtained as seed, from specialist firms, and may be grown fairly easily and cheaply to flowering size if one has normal patience and reasonable skill.

Semi-desert succulents
There is little need to give special advice for the growing of these plants. In brief, treatment should be a compromise between that advised for droughtland and desert species. The difference between droughtland and semi-desert is not large and neither is that between desert and semi-desert – at least in cultivation. In nature all these areas tend to shade into each other; growers will find it a great help to learn where their plants originate and which of them occur in similar, or even the same, stations.

Rain-forest succulents

Plants in this group are no more difficult to grow and flower than most droughtland species. Difficulties in cultivation usually arise from trying to accommodate them cheek by jowl with terrestrial cacti in the average 'cactus house'. They are then expected to put up with dry heat in summer and a long enforced winter rest, which even their neighbours on the bench often find trying. It is a strange fact that forest succulents are often to be seen at their best growing, not in the collections of succulent plant enthusiasts, but among house plants of all sorts, cared for by loving owners who sometimes do not even know that these particular plants are succulents. Treated as house plants many succulents from forest areas will do very well indeed, as long as they are not allowed to get too dry, especially those species which come from rain forests. Serious collectors frequently give plants in this group their own house, although it should not be difficult to divide a single greenhouse and provide a different environment in each part.

Rain forest succulents love and need humidity; they do not welcome even a short period of real dryness. In the wild the 'dry' period which such plants undergo is still a humid one. The rainfall may slacken or cease altogether for a while, but there is usually mist or fog to take its place until the rains return. Even if this does not happen, the water stored in the ground of a rain forest would supply humidity for a while and the overhead tree canopy would do much to prevent evaporation.

Most forest succulents continue to grow, more or less, throughout the year. Under glass or in the home these plants will benefit from frequent spraying and there is no need to worry if water remains on them afterwards; in fact it will be beneficial for them. On hot days it is a good plan to hose down the greenhouse interior and leave the floor really wet.

Epiphytic succulents often flower more profusely if their roots are cramped. To compensate for this they should be given plenty of nourishment and those which grow most strongly should be stood in saucers of water, to which feed may be added. Enough water should be given to keep the compost moist all the time, but not wet. When conditions suit them, some plants will grow aerial roots and if these are able to reach nourishment they will help to build much healthier plants. Such extra roots can be encouraged by growing plants, with or without pots, in plunge beds of compost, peat, powdered bark or moss. They may even appear if the plants, in their pots, are stood on wet gravel, in shallow trays.

A more decorative way of growing jungle plants is to stand them or hang them against a background of bark or moss, which may be held in place by wire or plastic netting. Smaller epiphytic species can be grown on natural branches or 'trees' of netting, stuffed with moss. Under the favourable conditions which these different methods provide, forest plants may make almost phenomenal growth and often show a true character which is not seen when they are given ordinary pot treatment.

Jungle cacti, and those other succulents which share their tastes, come from a wide range of forested habitats in various parts of the world. Growing them all together makes compromise necessary, as it does with the droughtland types, but this is not a difficult problem to overcome. Forest plants are generally tough, although they prefer not to tolerate as wide a temperature differential as droughtland and desert types. For safety it might be best to keep the temperature at night up to 45°F–50°F (7°C–10°C) although many species are safe down to five degrees lower, or even less, if the following day is a warm one. If direct sunlight is avoided daytime temperatures may rise as high as 80°F (27°C).

A number of forest species enjoy climbing up into bright heat and sometimes flower much better if they are encouraged to do so (hoyas and ceropegias are typical examples). But, like some of the popular garden climbers which have the same preference (clematis and wisterias, among others) they like to have their roots in cool shade. Stronger growing hoyas and other vining succulents should have their pots stood on the floor of the greenhouse where possible, and be trained up the greenhouse frame to display them to the best effect. It is even possible, if species of a similar habit but from different genera are chosen, to have their vines growing about each other, in a sort of stranded rope, which will give a variety of blooms over an extended season.

The compost for forest succulents should be more nourishing than the standard one for the general collection and should incorporate more organic material. Leafmould is very valuable if it can be obtained. Drainage is not so vitally important, although it should still be good and the compost porous. Epiphytic succulents are often grown in hanging pots and if the ambient air is humid enough they will give a good account of themselves and add a character of their own to the collection. Hangers should be made of strong wire or fine chain. There are very attractive hangers made of string or plastic which will often rot. It can be annoying not to be aware of these things until, one day, the hanger collapses and a special plant lies in pieces on the floor or on top of a benched specimen, particularly if a hand-made pot adds its own wreckage to the destruction. The plastic-coated garden wire sold in garden shops is strong and neat and serves very well for pots which are not too heavy.

To reduce the weight of any pot much of the sand or grit in a compost could be replaced by such materials as perlite or small-grade charcoal. The latter ingredient is very suitable for epiphytic plants.

For the most part this group of succulents contains easily grown, even rampant species, but there are some which need more care. They are usually small and slow growing, many are new to cultivation and all are greatly prized by collectors of jungle plants. Among the jungle cacti, plants of this sort will be found in such genera as *Rhipsalis, Rhipsalidopsis, Schlumbergera* and others. But this cactus group is still receiving attention from several taxonomists, each of whom needs to have his say. Therefore, expect names to be changed again, as they have already been changed more than once. Similar species with more permanent names will be found among the asclepiads, in such genera as *Ceropegia, Brachystelma* and so on.

These smaller epiphytes are not always easy to settle in; but if they do like their treatment they will usually grow well and even flower. The common problem in growing them is that just when these charming little plants seem to be past difficulty, and just when their owner begins to wonder why so much fuss is made over growing them, they will, with hardly any warning, rot off at the base or collapse into a heap of fragments. Why this happens is not always clear, even specialist collectors suffer from it. It may be caused by a physiological disorder of some sort. It is possibly the result of wet compost; these epiphytes like moisture but not too much of it, especially around their necks.

One consolation is that many of the shed pieces of plant, joints of stems or even side branches will be easy to root and become new plants. Many pieces may have grown adventitious roots already or may even have rooted down into the compost and become independent plants. It may well be that very wet conditions predispose a plant to indulge in what may be self-propagation. In natural conditions, the breaking up of an epiphyte would scatter pieces in all directions and some might well find a suitable place to grow. To add weight to this theory, it is quite possible to grow epiphytic succulents well by restricting one's attentions to frequent spraying and foliar feeding, as long as the ambient air is always humid and the compost slightly moist.

It is quite common for many succulents to root new growth as it is made and then gradually allow the old centre to die away. Epiphytes are not the only example of this habit. The stronger species of *Rhipsalis, Epiphyllum* and the like also drop sections of branches or stems, which make excellent cuttings, but then so do other terrestrial succulents. Probably the whole problem, even if it is infuriating to gardeners, is natural and to be expected. Our plants may have a perfect normal urge to exchange old sections of themselves for vigorous new ones. Would that we could be as fortunate!

Forest succulents almost certainly need to be shaded from direct sunlight. Once this is done the light level can be as high as it likes. A temporary summer wash of green, or preferably white, provides one good method of shielding succulents. Plastic sheeting, too, is now a popular precaution. It is often put into position to try it out for its heat retaining powers during the winter, then left in position, partly because of the bother in taking it down, but also because of its ability to shade through the rest of the year. Unfortunately, as always, there is one snag; greenhouses which are lined in this way not only keep the heat in, but also keep it out when the day is sunny. Even in summer they take much longer to warm up each day.

Perhaps the best solution is to use a lightweight plastic netting. This, if fixed to slide along horizontal wires at its top and bottom, can easily be drawn back on dull days. It also brings a second benefit; if it is drawn across at night in winter it will greatly help to reduce heat loss.

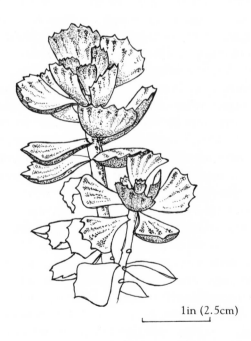

1in (2.5cm)

Kalanchoe rhombo-pilosum, a charming dwarf from Madagascar, where it usually grows ephiphytically. In cultivation it accepts pot conditions, but is never easy to grow well for very long. It will probably do best if treated as one of the smaller schlumbergeras or epiphyllanthus and watered with care. Several forms exists, in shades of green or grey, which are sometimes, as in the variation illustrated, beautifully marked.

Dry-forest succulents

There is little to add to the advice outlined in the previous section. Treatment for these succulents should be approximately pitched between that needed for droughtland species and that for rain forest types. Once again, it always helps if one can find out details of natural habitats; such knowledge is invaluable for providing the right clues to a plant's proper management.

In simple terms the differences between a wet forest and a dry one are: the dry forest will be less humid, may have more open growth of trees and other plants and will not have a close tree canopy. There will almost certainly be a greater drop in temperature at night, especially at a high altitude, and there will probably be a definitely drier period at some time in a typical year.

The stapeliads

It is debatable whether the stapeliads with their strange carrion flowers are the most fascinating group of succulents. Even their strongest supporters could not deny that they can also be the most infuriating group in any collection. Whatever the species and however well it may appear to be growing, just when one is least expecting it, the wretched plant will succumb to rot and collapse into a pile of mushy pieces. It is not simply that stapeliads are difficult to grow and flower. Most of them, if not exactly beginners' plants, are easy enough to cultivate – for a while, that is. It is their impermanence as members of the collection which brings the problems, problems just as great for the experienced specialist as for anybody else. Nevertheless, the group is too intriguing and its flowers too beautiful for it to be abandoned. One must do what one can to satisfy these fickle plants. While they are with us they will give us a great deal of pleasure.

Like all succulent plants, stapeliads need porous soil and good drainage, but for them it is doubly important. There is much to be said for providing a nourishing layer of compost at the bottom of the pot or pan in which they are to be grown and then filling up with a second, deeper layer of nothing but drainage material. In this way only the ends of the plants' roots are actually in contact with the compost. Stapeliads grow in the shade of other vegetation, and do not like direct sunlight, especially in hot weather. A reasonable amount of water is necessary during their active season for healthy growth and flowering. Regular re-potting is advised and all stapeliads should have the benefit of an occasional watering with a dose of systemic insecticide and fungicide. Root health is most important and the root growth which is closest to and therefore underneath the plant body is very susceptible to fungal attack and mealy bugs. It is therefore important that they should be inspected frequently.

Most stapeliads grow as small, multi-stemmed bushes or as prostrate carpeters. For this reason pans are more suitable than narrow pots. New stems grow outwards from the centre and are very likely to root themselves down into the compost. Once the younger stems are well rooted it is always a wise precaution to detach them from the older, central growth. This should be done by making two downward, vertical cuts into the connecting part of the stem and removing the slice so made. The cut ends should be allowed to dry, then dusted with a fungicide. Once independent, the young stem will soon grow into a new plant. Using this method may eventually provide several thriving young plants growing around the original one, which could then be discarded as it will be past its prime and unlikely to flower again. A small colony of this sort is a very good insurance aganst the ills which stapeliads are heir to. If one of them does strike, it will be unlikely to affect every one of the young plants. In any case it is often possible to save a stem or side branch by grafting it onto a ceropegia tuber, for example.

It is hoped that this section will not dissuade anybody from growing stapeliads. A succulent collection is incomplete if it does not include one or two at least, and nowhere else in the succulent plant world can such flowers be found.

Caudiciform succulents

Caudiciforms are mostly new to cultivation, and they possess a double adaptation to their environment in that both the perennial and the annual parts of the plant share the task of surviving. A caudiciform succulent is so called because it has a caudex, which is either an enlarged root, a swollen stem, or sometimes a combination of both. The caudex stores food or water against periods of shortage, and it grows at ground level, above it, or partly or completely buried below ground. The latter position is of special value for survival in areas where periodic fires or predators might destroy any exposed growth.

In its natural habitat the growth made above ground is usually annual or semi-perennial. Typical annual growth takes the form of a vine which may bear leaves and which has the task of flowering and fruiting during the rainy season, whose commencement starts it into growth. The vine is also able (by photosynthesis) to produce the all-important nourishment which the caudex must hold in reserve during the drier part of the year when the vine has ripened its fruits, produced its seed and died down.

Not only does this double adaptation have a functional purpose in nature; it also has a twofold aesthetic value for collectors. It is the usual practice for caudiciform succulents to be grown with the caudex, or part of it, exposed above the compost. In this position, which the plants submit to with good grace, the beauty of the caudex may be enjoyed as well as that of the annual growth. What is more, the trickier species may be grown much more safely in this way, as they will be less in danger from rot. Some die-hard growers have objected to caudiciform plants being included in collections, though there is no logical reason why they should not be. Their dual function and their individual cycles of growth make the caudiciform species unique among succulent plants. To be comprehensive every collection should contain a few. The very varied caudexes offer real beauty and the vines, together with their flowers and fruits, provide a rich choice of form and colour.

Wherever a collector's special enthusiasms take him there will probably be caudiciform species to be discovered. They are not exclusive to any one genus or even to one family of succulents and may be found among euphorbias, asclepiads, pelargoniums, tylecodons, and elsewhere. Some of these plants may be easily and quickly raised from seed. The traffic in imported, often smuggled plants should not be supported by any plant lover worthy of the name, and in most cases these specimens from the wild are battered or mutilated, with dry bodies and little or no roots. Often they prove impossible to resuscitate, and they cannot compare with plants raised in cultivation from seed or cuttings.

Caudiciform succulents are not, for the most part, difficult to grow, although some slower growing kinds, pachypodiums eg, will not flower until maturity. The invariable problem is that the grower cannot always be sure what caudiciforms want to do. Sometimes it is difficult not to believe that the plants themselves are unsure about it all. Even specimens of the same species will decide to rest or grow individually and choose a different time of year for their active season. They may even shorten or prolong it without rhyme or reason. Three specimens of *Testudinaria elephantipes* in the writer's possession, seed-raised and now displaying impressive caudexes, have through the years all pursued independent lives. At any one time all three may be showing different stages of growth. One must always be quick to notice when caudiciforms signal their needs.

Leaves falling or yellowing should indicate that the growing season is drawing to its close, particularly if flowers have appeared and even more surely if fruit has ripened. In the same way, a flush of colour on the plant body, the slight swelling of growth points or the appearance of a green vine tip are equally clear signs that the season's growth is beginning. First waterings should always be made cautiously, even though one may know that a particular species, in its natural habitat, may begin its growing season as the result of a flash flood which leaves it standing in water. Spraying alone may suffice to bring a greenhouse specimen into growth, until sufficient progress has been made for water to be given freely.

It has sometimes been advised, although surely not by growers, that they should be given 'less than average' water when the annual growths are being made and none at all when the plants are resting. Such advice is difficult to accept if one considers the climate of the various regions in which succulents of this sort are to be found. Healthy top growth can only be made if generous treatment is provided while it is being made. The rate of growth of vines on some caudiciform plants is extraordinary, especially with mature plants. Of course it is true that such desert species as the geophytic euphorbias which are not vining, need very great care and limited nourishment at all times. Such species as the cyphostemmas, jatrophas, fouquierias and testudinarias will take up as much water as they can be given, once they are in active growth, and this treatment should be safe, unless a cold, dull period intervenes. We have to remember that all the annual growth, together with flowering and fruiting may, in nature, have to be made very quickly during what may be a short rainy season.

During their rest period, when annual growths have died down, caudiciforms must be kept almost dry. But the important word is 'almost'; some specimens which have been allowed to dry right out may not revive again, however persuaded.

Madagascan succulents

During recent years, the island of Madagascar (Malagasy Republic) has enriched succulent plant collections in many other parts of the world with a number of exciting new species. It is a pity that pachypodiums have been the ones to attract most attention, as there have also been charming, dwarf aloes, ceropegias, cynanchums, many new euphorbias and much else. Perhaps it is not surprising that most of these wonderful new succulents have been, if not overvalued, at least overpriced. Imported specimens, often without roots and with little chance of surviving, have been sold for more than their worth, when the same species have been available, green and growing, for considerably less, from American and European nurseries. The worst aspect of this situation has been that certain Madagascan habitats have been robbed of slow growing, rare plants. After a very short time in island establishments, these have been sold into the trade as nursery-grown specimens.

Sadly, few British nurseries have propagated these new species, simple as most of them are to increase, as it has been too easy to import collected plants, which are often in very poor condition when offered for sale and have little chance of surviving especially in the hot dry cactus conditions waiting for most of them. As a result they have gained a reputation for difficulty which is generally undeserved.

It would be sheer folly to introduce such a treasure as *Euphorbia lophogona* into a greenhouse whose small environment has been planned to suit a collection of terrestrial cacti. This euphorbia is actually quite easy to cultivate and flower, and to propagate – either from the seed which it so readily produces or from cuttings. It will not survive hot dry air and direct sunlight, nor will it take kindly to getting too cold in winter or too dry. Treatment of this sort would endanger or kill most forest succulents. In its natural habitat, *Euphorbia lophogona* can expect about 60in (150cm) of rain in a year. During a three month 'dry' period fog and heavy mists provide moisture.

There are Madagascan indigenes which have been grown in cultivation for many years, so much so that they have even acquired popular names, which is not the case with many succulents. *Euphorbia milii v. splendens*, the 'Crown of Thorns'; and *Kalanchoe tomentosa*, the 'Panda Plant', are two such old favourites; and the lovely weeds, once known as bryophyllums – *Kalanchoe daigremontiana*, the 'Mexican Hat Plant' and its relatives – are widespread in collections or on windowsills in a score of countries.

With some exceptions, a few of the aloe species and the pachypodiums, succulents from Madagascar are forest plants. Treated as such, most are easy enough to grow and propagate. There are conscienti-

1in (2.5cm)

Aloe antandroi, another of the charming Madagascan species with attractive form and flowers. This is a slowish growing species which in the wild makes a shrub up to 3ft (1m) in height, with its stems partly supported by surrounding vegetation. The flowers open to bright red, often in winter.

ous growers, mindful of their specimens real need, who have gone to the other extreme from the cactus collectors and given the plants special conditions. Installed in 'hot boxes' (greenhouses within greenhouses) Madagascans have been given a humid environment where the temperature is usually not varied and is kept to a minimum of something like 60°F (15°C) constantly. For a time the pampered darlings have prospered and have grown large and lush. Then, inevitably, a decline has set in and, when they have succumbed, they have left a little more evidence of their supposed difficulty to grow behind them.

A 'hot box' is a very satisfactory way of growing tropical forest plants, but it is essential to maintain a temperature cycle, if they are to stay healthy and grow as they should. A night-time temperature of 50°F (10°C) seems to satisfy most Madagascan succulents and some will be safe at 45°F (7°C) or even 40°F (5°C). During the daytime, an increase up to 80°F (27°C), with good humidity maintained for the rain forest species, should help to provide a suitable variation for the plants' well-being.

Of course, temperature and humidity are not everything. Madagascan succulents will grow for most of the year and some will flower over a long period if they do so. During all this time water and nourishment may be given generously. With care and intelligent management, most of these very individual, sometimes odd, but always lovely Madagascans should be no more trouble than the average crassula or epiphyllum.

Rosette succulents

For horticultural purposes these are well worth considering as a group. Most of them are not difficult to grow and flower; and, when they are taken together, it is possible to find similarities and problems shared by the plants of very different genera. Included here are a few plants which are not usually regarded as rosette succulents; nevertheless, in gardening terms this is where they best belong.

A rosette is a rose-like cluster or circle of leaves which is found at the top of a plant body, stem or branch. Most succulent rosette plants belong to one genus or another of the family Crassulaceae, to such genera as *Crassula, Dudleya, Echeveria, Sedum* and others. Many hybrids between both species and genera (as well as between cultivars) exist and as they may be produced quite easily we have been given a large number of beautiful hybrid plants with which to brighten our greenhouses all the year round.

Rosette plants may also be found in the Liliaceae, among the species of *Gasteria, Haworthia* and *Aloe* (with hybrids also existing) and among members of the *Agavaceae*.

Some rosette plants form stems; some grow flat on the soil or against the surface of rocks or cliff faces. All increase by multiplying into mounds or clumps, or by forming new rosettes on stolons or stems (as well as by seed). Some species, eg, many of the sedums, grow as leaf-clad stems which bear terminal rosettes, the stems often dropping old leaves progressively and remaining bare. Other rosette plants, notably some aeoniums, form stems which branch and bear terminal rosettes, the

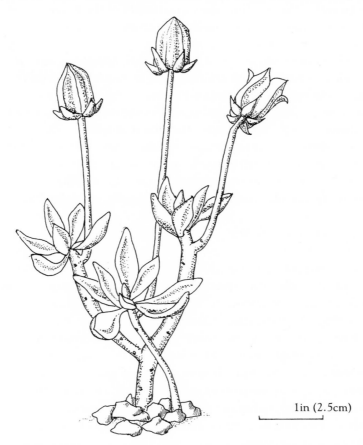

1in (2.5cm)

Echeveria harmsii, an old favourite, often sold by florists as a house plant, and still known by many people under its old name of *Oliveranthus elegans*. This species grows as an erect sub-shrub and carries solitary, bright-scarlet flowers which are the largest of all the echeveria species.

stems becoming woody until a tree-like adult plant is made. If detached, leaves of many rosette succulents will bud at the point where they previously joined their stem, then root and usually produce a new rosette.

The typical ground hugging, stemless rosette succulent is always in danger of rotting if excess water is given, especially if any is allowed to remain in the rosette itself. Spraying is of benefit to nearly all succulents, but it is best not to spray stemless rosettes, nor to water them overhead. If shortage of time makes this necessary, or if water should accidentally find its way into a rosette it should be removed. One of the large wash brushes used in watercolour painting is the ideal tool and one could be kept close to a collection of rosette plants at all times, just for safety's sake. If a leak should develop in a greenhouse roof, it will inevitably drip on to one of the touchiest species.

All rosette plants are most secure if they are given very deep drainage around their necks and if dead or dying leaves are regularly removed from beneath the rosette (a pair of forceps could be kept next to the wash brush). Plants which clump or mound, particularly those known to be extra-sensitive to surplus water, may be grown raised above the top of the pot. If three or four pieces of stone (tufa is ideal, if it can be obtained) are set in a rough circle, the rosette may be set in their centre and the space left filled with grit. At first this may not look very attractive but soon the plant will send new feeding roots into the grit, while the deeper ones will pull it down into position. Eventually, the parent plant will form new rosettes, or divide itself and spill over the edges of its raised bed, covering the circle of stones from view and displaying itself to perfection.

The leaves of rosette plants are often covered with a waxy bloom, or with a felty one of coarse or fine hairs. Other species may possess leaves which are powdered heavily. The beautiful appearance of such leaves is easily spoiled which gives another reason for not allowing water to remain on them. By the same token, any chemicals used upon rosette succulents should be given from below and care should be taken to make sure that there is no drift when sprays or aerosols are being used nearby. If tiny pests are seen between the leaves of this type of plant it will sometimes prove impossible to remove them without damage. Once again, treatment should be given from below, preferably with one of the new systematic insecticides which make plants so unappetising to their predators. One old-fashioned precaution is still a good one, and that is to sprinkle a few grains of paradichlorbenzene (sold as a moth preventive) under each plant.

There are succulents which may usefully be considered as rosette plants even if they are not usually thought of as such. Nobody talks of 'rosette' euphorbias, for example, and yet it is convenient, perhaps even wise, to treat the 'Medusa Head' species as if they were. Euphorbias in this group all possess a central body (or caudex) often shaped like a carrot, from which radiate a number of side stems or arms. The bodies of these euphorbias are best protected from too much wet with a deep layer of grit and, as with the real rosette succulents, it is best not to allow surplus water to remain on the crown of the plant. Few of these plants, if any, will have a bloom on this crown and it is a good idea to give the plant a fine misting occasionally, especially when flower buds are seen.

There are also mesems which are best treated as rosette plants; their appearance will suggest which. A number of the dwarf species grow terminal bunches of leaves which may rot if they remain wet for too long but which benefit from light spraying if all surplus water is afterwards removed.

From time to time other succulents may be encountered which suggest, by their appearance, that they should be given 'rosette' treatment. If so, the recommendations outlined in this section should be followed.

Winter growers

A myth persists that cacti, and by inference all other succulents, grow during our northern summer and then rest in winter. We are sometimes told that those which do not, the Christmas cactus is usually given as the chief example, follow a different cycle because 'they are not true cacti'. The pity is that this nonsense is, quite naturally, accepted by beginners. It seems impossible to believe that it should still be followed by those who actually grow succulent plants – or at least cacti. Yet, so it is.

Like seaside amusement arcades, cactus houses are usually shut down by the end of September. The unfortunate occupants are left to sleep, and the houses themselves neglected and not even visited regularly during the colder months, except to check the heating. Some growers do not even visit their greenhouses for days, or weeks, at a time during the winter. Succulents may even survive such treatment (especially mesems and terrestrial cacti) and this is accepted by growers as justification of their methods. Rather, it is evidence of the plants' own toughness and resistance.

For some reason or other, cactus growers seem to want to be rid of their hobby between the onset of autumn and the arrival of spring, during a time of year when the greenhouse could still show a fine display of colour and interest. From October onward plants are kept as cold and dry as possible until spring and otherwise ignored. This kill or cure policy means that those plants which perish can be labelled 'difficult' and those which submit and survive can take their place among the 'real' cacti. It is quite true that, under this form of treatment, some succulents will not only adapt and learn to grow, but even flower to suit us in summertime. Yet few of these converts will do as well as they might and many of the 'difficult' species are not at all difficult if given correct management.

It is, fortunately, simple enough to find out which succulents are winter growers. Proper observation of one's own specimens is the most important guide, assisted by reference books which give information about natural habitats. Such valuable books as *Succulents In the Veld*, by Rolf Rawé (now out of print, but indispensable if a copy can be found) or Doreen Court's *Succulent Flora of Southern Africa* contain many facts concerning the distribution of succulents in that part of the world as well as information on climate, weather and rainfall patterns.

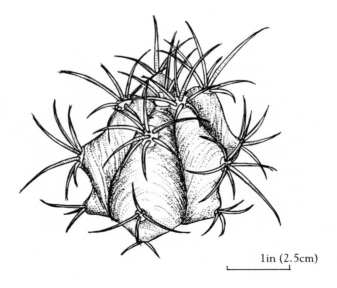

1in (2.5cm)

Echinocactus palmeri, a cactus from northern Mexico. It has strong yellow spines, the central one of which is thickened, with a brown base. In its natural habitat the species may reach 6ft (2m) in height; as a pot specimen it grows more slowly and modestly.

Most of the winter succulents in cultivation come, as it happens, from the western side of southern Africa. To their number belong such small species as the 'mimicry' mesems (the lithops, conophytums and their like), quite a few crassulas, some anacampseros, euphorbias and pelargoniums, together with other species from such genera as tylecodon and many more. It could also be the case that some stapeliads – those tricky but desirable succulents which try the patience of the most skilful cultivator – would do better if treated as winter growers.

There are other succulent plants which, even if they are not winter growers in the strictest sense, appear to want to be more active at this period than in the heat of summer. Yet, on the other hand, it could be argued that their ceasing to grow at this time is simply their reaction to our long, hot, inhibiting summer days. Most species from the Canary Islands are accommodating enough; but they seem to want a short midsummer rest and to be kept growing for the rest of the year. Some of the tree aeoniums from this Mediterranean area will indicate their need to go more or less dormant by dropping the outer leaves of their rosettes, which they tighten up into a ball or a flat disc. *Aeonium simsii*, a non-stem forming species, dries up into a very dead looking ball of chaff. Its appearance at the warmest time of year may well have lead to its being thrown away on more than one occasion. However, deep down in the centre of each rosette will be found a persistent tiny green point of growth, which soon enlarges to produce a bright clump which is as good as new.

Echeveria growers would probably agree that their collections reach a peak of colour before the end of winter. The best months are usually February or March, especially if the winter is a sunny one. Many species and hybrids are in bloom or bud at this time of the year, as will be dudleyas and other members of the Crassulaceae, haworthias and dwarf aloes. A few euphorbias, senecios and, of course, many mesems will also be busily flowering and brightening the impatient days during which we wait for spring.

The argument is occasionally put forward that it costs too much to allow succulents to grow in winter. It is odd that collectors who will spend large sums of money on large specimen plants do not, it seems, think so favourably of spending a reasonable amount on caring for them properly. Yet winter growing does not have to cost so much, particularly for desert or droughtland succulents. These species will, as already stated, stand much lower night-time temperatures than used to be thought. Many of them will live happily through the winter in a much lower temperature than they enjoy at other times of the year, and they will also flower.

The important thing for winter growers is not to allow them to become absolutely dry, however cold the temperature may be. This will possibly sound like the greatest heresy of all but it is worth repeating. No succulents, not even the mesems and terrestrial cacti, should ever, at any time, be allowed to dry out completely. Drying out a succulent, compost and roots as well, will send it into dormancy and run the risk of it not waking up again when you want it to.

In their natural habitat, even the terrestrial cacti and mesems such as lithops and conophytums probably receive a little moisture during their dry periods. This can come as an unexpected shower of rain, but much more likely as dew or mist, collected on spines or on the plant bodies themselves. It may be taken up by a plant's fine roots which run just below the surface of the ground. Other species, which may or may not undergo a period of complete water shortage in their natural home (and which may, as a result, not survive) should not be given a clear signal, by withholding water completely, that a drought period is upon them. A little moisture in the compost will keep them sufficiently active to continue growing and flowering, as they will do if given this bare amount of sustenance. On dull days, the provision of artificial light will help greatly to keep plants in this condition happy.

Species which are fully active during the winter months may be watered and fed more generously. They will probably not come to harm, although a little discretion should be used in such treatment if a period of extreme wet or cold comes along.

There are now so many succulents available to the keen collector who looks out for them, either as seed or grown specimens, that an unbroken succession of flowers and growth can be enjoyed all the year round. Collectors who do not keep their hobby alive all through the year are missing much that a little extra expense and attention could so easily bring.

Frerea indica enjoys the distinction of being the only stapeliad to have true leaves. This Indian species occurs naturally in the vicinity of waterfalls, where it trails its bright-green stems down wet rock faces. The flowers are chocolate brown, flecked with gold.

The Plants

ABROMEITIELLA (Bromeliaceae)

Low-growing cushion plants, native to the High Andes of Argentina and Bolivia, and composed of tightly clustering rosettes of spiny, triangular leaves. In their own habitat these charming little bromeliads form large mats; in cultivation their silvery hummocks are less ambitious and keep their miniature beauty within bounds, bearing small, sessile inflorescences and green flowers. These tiny, high mountain species are tough and very xerophytic.

Cultivation Desert or semi-desert. Little water and much light.
Propagation Seed if obtainable, or careful division.

ADANSONIA (Bombacaceae)

Adansonia digitata, the Baobab, is probably the largest of all succulent plants, at least in its African home. In a pot, however, it is most unlikely to reach its wild stature of over 50ft (17m) and, as a young plant, it will make an interesting addition to a caudiciform collection. Other species are found in Madagascar and Australia, but all are rare in cultivation.

Cultivation Droughtland.
Propagation Seed. A high temperature may be necessary to effect germination.

ADENIA (Passifloraceae)

Few specimens are seen in collections, although photographs of species taken in the wild suggest that these might be of interest, if only to caudiciform collectors – if they could be obtained. Almost any species is worth trying if seed should be offered. They will all remain a modest size in pots in the greenhouse.

Cultivation Droughtland. Not difficult in a bright position.
Propagation Seed although it should be possible to root cuttings of top growth.

ADENIUM (Apocynaceae)

Not to be confused with *Adenia.* This is also a genus of stem or caudiciform succulents, from dry steppe areas in a variety of African habitats. They are small plants, easy to grow, flower and propagate in cultivation. A generation or so ago, adeniums were rare in private collections. Now, even if not exactly common, they are seen much more often. Fortunately, the trade in imported specimens has been largely replaced by vegetative propagation or by seed raising. Today's captive plants not only look much better but grow more reliably as well. All species have attractive shapes, with nicely barked bodies and varied leaves. Flowers are displayed in small clusters at the tips of the stems, in shades of pink or red.

Cultivation Fairly easy. Warm droughtland to dry forest, plenty of light.
Propagation Simple from good undamaged seed, which should be plump.

ADROMISCHUS *(Crassulaceae)*
There are similarities between this genus and *Cotyledon,* in which it was once included. What is now called *Adromischus* is a genus of dwarf shrubs, from South Africa and Namibia with very succulent leaves and erect, tubular flowers on wiry stems. Sometimes dismissed as easy beginners' succulents, they are not always so easy to keep in prime condition over a long period of time. At their best adromischus deserve the highest praise for the beauty of their foliage, which is often conspicuously marked or mottled, even if the flowers are not very striking.

Naming is still a problem with the species in this genus and it seems that numerous forms and as many names, which really belong to a few dozen species at most, are all completely confused.

Cultivation Semi-desert. Avoid wet compost but spray. If adromischus prove difficult and lose their roots, as sometimes occurs, treat as winter growing, give good light and less water, preferably from below.
Propagation Simple. Any detached leaf will root. Seed may be obtainable for the less common species.

AEONIUM *(Crassulaceae)*
These rosette succulents are distributed principally in the Canary Islands, with some species in the Mediterranean area. They are easily grown, fairly hardy and range in size from tallish tree-like species, several feet in height, down to prostrate mats, with a variety of domed or flat-topped, much-branched shrubs in between the two extremes.

The flowers of aeoniums are small; but they are carried in racemes (which in the larger species may hold hundreds of blooms) in white, cream, pink or gold. Inflorescences grow terminally, from rosettes which die after flowering. Replacement rosettes usually grow from below the old one on side branches, and this regenerative habit may be encouraged by moving the plant into the shade, cutting off the dead flower spike, and watering and feeding well.

Like other Canary Island endemics, aeoniums appreciate a rest in late spring or early summer, during which time they should be kept fairly dry. Most species undergo a change in appearance while otherwise inactive. The outer leaves of the rosettes will die and fall, and what is left of the central part of them will tighten and flatten the remaining leaves, so that

Adromischus species, a South African genus which offers a variety of colourful, compact shrubs and shrublets for greenhouse cultivation. Most forms have attractively marked leaves.

1in (2.5cm)

they overlap into a flat disc. One or two of the more prostrate species tighten their rosettes into what appears to be a ball of dead leaves. *Aeonium simsii* seems to die right away and it becomes difficult to believe that the mound of dead chaff, which so recently was bright green and growing, is in fact still alive. But all these changes are natural and will re-serve themselves when the dormant period ends.

Cultivation Droughtland. Not too warm; most species are coast dwellers by nature – all will enjoy a summer spell in the garden.
Propagation Seed or rosette cuttings.

AGAVE (*Agavaceae*)
Agaves come from tropical and subtropical America and the genus num-bers approximately one hundred species. As flowering is terminal and does not occur until a plant is large and mature, agaves grown in pots should not be considered as flowering plants. Nevertheless, they are, even without flowers, beautiful and varied. The hard-leaved species are almost hardy, especially the forms of *Agave americana,* and some will even grow out of doors in the warmer parts of the British Isles, until a really hard winter comes along. Even then, some plants will survive.

Some agaves rapidly become too large for small greenhouses and have to be discarded, though there are a number which will leave replacement offsets behind them. Collectors with little space should look for such small wonders as A. *victoriae-reginae* or A. *parviflora.*

Cultivation Droughtland. Very effective if stood in the garden during the warmer months. Favourite species, known to grow too large, may be held back by under-potting and root pruning, which does no harm.
Propagation Seed is obtainable for many species. Offsets, if not already rooted, will do so easily.

AICHRYSON (*Crassulaceae*)
A small genus from the Atlantic islands, similar to the smaller, shrubby aeoniums and sometimes included with them. One popular species exists, A. *domesticum,* usually seen in its attractive, variegated form, which makes a good house plant, in a good light. Flowers are yellow and abundant.

Cultivation Droughtland. Easy to grow.
Propagation Seed or rosette cuttings.

ALLUAUDIA *(Didiereaceae)*
In their native, south-west Madagascar (Malagasy Republic), alluaudias
grow as tall shrubs or trees, among other vegetation, and are the haunt of
some of the island's remaining lemur species, in spite of the very spiny
stems. Alluaudias are leafless or else bear pairs of small, bright green
leaves. They are on the borderline of succulence and should rather be
thought of as dry forest xerophytes. Flowers, when produced, are small.

In the greenhouse, alluaudias make handsome specimens, particularly
effective when they have made good, branched growth (which can be
encouraged by cutting back) and can display their fine, silvery trunks in a
6–7in (15–17cm) pot.

Cultivation Dry forest. Not difficult.
Propagation Stem cuttings, well sealed or calloused, will root in
warmth.

ALLUAUDIOPSIS *(Didiereaceae)*
The one species is separated from *Alluaudia* by reason of small, botanical
differences. Treatment should be the same as that given to the preceding
genus.

ALOE *(Liliaceae)*
Aloes comprise a very large genus of rosette succulents, both stemless
and tall growing. They have a very wide distribution in South Africa,
North Africa, Arabia and Madagascar (Malagasy Republic). Aloes differ
from agaves (to which they often bear a superficial resemblance) mainly
by virtue of the fact that they flower laterally. A lateral inflorescence
does not end the life of the plant or the rosette which produces it, which
means that in the case of the many aloes which flower readily, we can
enjoy the blooms, and sometimes the scent, year after year.

The genus includes a number of dwarf and small species, mostly from
Madagascar or East Africa, which, however long we grow them, will not
outgrow a small pot or pan. They need a little more care than the larger,
more vigorous species. If they are kept active for most of the year, including winter, these appealing miniature plants will bloom well and may
flower more than once in the year.

Cultivation Easy enough for all species which are generally obtainable.
The dwarf Madagascans need good drainage and more attention, but are

not very difficult if their real needs are understood. As these aloes tend to pull themselves down into their compost during the hottest time of year (their resting period), it is important to check that this action has not compacted the mixture too greatly. It should, if this has occurred, be loosened up before winter sets in.

Propagation Seed or offsets. Offset cuttings of most species root well and fairly quickly.

ALOINOPSIS *(Mesembryanthemaceae)*

Dwarf, tufted plants with tuberous rootstocks, charming and necessary to any collection of small mesems. There is a close affinity with the genus *Nananthus* and some botanists prefer to combine both genera. Both in commerce and cultivation there is much confusion over naming. These are valuable plants in the greenhouse, not only for the beauty of their form and foliage, but especially for the lovely winter flowers.

Cultivation Desert or semi-desert. Winter growers and not very difficult to maintain and flower. Those species most likely to be called *Nananthus* by taxonomists are those which originate from the northern and more arid part of the whole combined distribution area in South Africa. It is also pointed out sometimes that a few species prefer additional lime in their compost, but in practice all of them seem amenable to sharing similar treatment.

The possession of large, tuberous roots makes very deep drainage advisable. Alternatively these plants may be grown as caudiciform succulents, with the roots raised above the compost. Very, very good light should be the rule if aloinopsis species are to look natural. Only the tuberculate area of each leaf should be visible, the plain portion of the surface should be hidden, not easy to achieve in northern countries. A high intensity of fluorescent light might help to obtain it.

Propagation Seed or cuttings. Seedlings may flower in their first year.

ANACAMPSEROS *(Portulacaceae)*

No matter how small the greenhouse, room should be made for a few of these dainty little plants, from the most arid parts of South Africa and Namibia. The genus is divided into two main groups: the section *Anacampseros* contains plants with very fleshy leaves of dark green, brown or reddish-brown, which often have bristly hairs in their axils; the section *Avonia* has slender stems covered with papery stipules which completely hide the minute green leaves and which resemble the scales of a fish. In both sections the inflorescences are terminal and the flowers have five petals, some blooms being cleistogamous, that is, they are able to set seed without opening. In general, the flowers of the *Anacampseros* section species are richly pink, red or purple, while *Avonia* flowers are usually white or pale coloured. In both sections flowers will open only in very bright light and they last for no more than a few hours.

Avonia section species are unique among succulents. When grown in a very good light, the stipules of the stems become white or silvery and the plants often resemble bird droppings. The whitest species are usually found growing in white quartz, which helps to conceal them. Stipules on the stems of these plants catch and hold the heavy, nocturnal dews which are often the plants' only means of survival in those areas which are largely rainless.

Cultivation *Anacampseros* section species are not difficult to grow. One even sees them grown as house plants and surviving, although their appearance, when they are so indulged, gives little indication of the real beauty which is theirs by right. *Avonia* section species, on the other hand, will put up with very little abuse. Most are winter growers and during this time they require light spraying and possibly a little water from below. These plants are not easy to grow well and always need careful treatment in a good light and in fast draining compost. They are, however, deserving of every effort to satisfy their demands.

Propagation Seed for both sections. Cuttings of *Anacampseros* species will root. Cuttings of *Avonia* species may do so.

APOROCACTUS *(Cactaceae)*

Aporocactus flagelliformis is the well known 'Rat's Tail Cactus' and is the type species of this small genus of Mexican epiphytes. Other species are not hard to come by and all are fine plants for a hanging basket or a high shelf, positions which will display their long slender stems and their attractive spines to the best advantage, and enhance the lovely pink of the flowers which the warm spring days usually bring in such profusion.

There are now a number of fine hybrids between *Aporocactus* species and other epicacti and these are equally beautiful, in or out of flower. They are identified by the prefix X *Aporo-*, and all varieties flower abundantly, usually in shades of orange, rose or red. The flowers themselves are smaller than those of the so-called 'Orchid' epiphyllums, but have much more style and grace than most of them.

Cultivation As for all jungle cacti. Easy to grow and flower, but too much shade will cause stems to etiolate and spines to lose colour. Aporocactus and their hybrids appreciate generous treatment and are fairly hardy; they like to grow for most of the year.

Propagation Easy from seed or from cuttings, preferably of whole stems, the short ones which grow from the centre of a clump being the best to use.

APTENIA *(Mesembryanthemaceae)*
A genus of only two species, which grow in the eastern coastal areas of South Africa, sometimes in brackish conditions. The plants form extensive mats of heart-shaped leaves, with small, reddish-purple flowers in abundance. The variegated form of A. *cordifolia* is the one usually seen.

Cultivation Simple mesem. Does well in the garden during summer and flowers better for the air and exposure. Colonies have now naturalised themselves in the main Channel Islands, the Jersey form being slightly larger in its parts, with redder and larger flowers.

Propagation Seed or cuttings.

ARGYRODERMA *(Mesembryanthemaceae)*
These are the delightful little 'Silver Skins', a small genus which has been further reduced by one taxonomist to about ten species. Names, therefore, in specialist seed and plant lists are likely to conflict. Argyrodermas are highly adapted, dwarf mesems which consist of one pair of leaves and which bear brilliant, solitary flowers in white, purple or yellow.

The genus comes from the western Cape and is winter growing. One species, at least, should be included in any collection of dwarf mesems.

Cultivation As for similar desert mesems. Even when they are active these plants should be given no more water than is necessary to keep them unwrinkled; too much will split them and spoil the year's growth. Argyrodermas need a very light position to bring out the pale beauty which gives them their popular name.

Propagation Easy from seed. Most species are obtainable.

ARIOCARPUS (Cactaceae)

In spite of the free availability of seed and the fact that seedlings are as readily obtainable, these true desert cacti continue to be regarded as rare plants, especially now that the trade in imported wildlings has declined. Ariocarpus are extremely slow growing and are for this reason usually grafted when young seedlings. Yet, even though this practice brings them through their most vulnerable period more quickly they are never in a hurry to increase their size. Ariocarpus are plants with an individual, perhaps one could say aristocratic character, which all cactus lovers should try to accommodate.

Native to Northern Mexico and part of Texas, ariocarpus are top-shaped and grow with their bodies pulled well down into the soil. They are covered, on their upper surface, with hard, horny tubercles and no spines are present. Flowers are funnel-shaped and may be carmine, pink or yellowish, according to species.

Cultivation These are real desert cacti and they should not be treated too generously. Nevertheless, when they are growing they will take good watering. Most of the specimens seen are under-watered and look as if they are dead; the sight of a live plant, in flower and actually showing green growth is a revelation. In the greenhouse a hot sunny position is necessary and a good winter rest, during which time hardly any water at all should be given, ie, only enough to prevent death or desiccation.

Propagation From seed, until methods of micro-propagation are developed. Seed is usually available and viable. With such slow growing succulents as these, the early days of life are the most difficult. Seedlings should have bright light and every other encouragement to overcome the inevitable competition of mosses or algal growths. Tiny plants should be kept growing throughout their first two or three years.

ASTROLOBA (Liliaceae)

A small genus, very close to *Haworthia* and restricted in its distribution to the south of the Cape Province. All species are short-stemmed and form a dense covering of hard, spine-tipped leaves, arranged in five ranks. The flowers are similar to those of the haworthias.

Cultivation As for haworthias. Half shade or broken sunlight is ideal.

Propagation Seed or cuttings of detached stems, which usually root with no trouble.

ASTROPHYTUM *(Cactaceae)*

A very small and very individual genus of Mexican cacti, which are easy to grow and flower and fairly resistant to cold. They are remarkable for the covering of white flecks which their surface displays; in some forms this is complete, in some absent and in others patterned in decorative zones. Some species are spineless and some have their bodies almost hidden by long curved spines, which give the plants the look of a bird's nest. The flowers are showy and variable, yellow to gold and sometimes showing red in the throat.

Cultivation Semi-desert, Simple.
Propagation Seed.

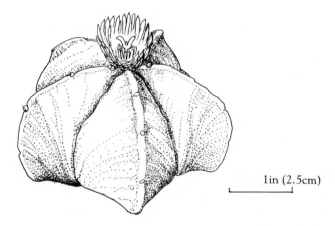

1in (2.5cm)

Astrophytum myriostigma, a spineless cactus from Mexico. Its body is unique among cacti, being covered with white flecks which in good light give the plant a snowlike appearance. The freely produced flowers are satiny yellow and up to 2in (6cm) or more in diameter.

AZTEKIUM *(Cactaceae)*

One species only, *Aztekium ritteri,* exists; but this is one of the most easily recognisable of all cacti. It has a turnip-shaped root and grows as a small flat-headed dull-green globe, with a depressed woolly crown. The plant body has deep ribs, which are pleated horizontally; there are no spines. The flowers are pink to white and tiny. Very slow growing.

Cultivation Difficult (see the notes on Ariocarpus). This is another true desert cactus.
Propagation Seed. Germination is not difficult. After-care is exceedingly so.

BERGERANTHUS *(Mesembryanthemaceae)*

Easy, dwarf clumpers, most of them from the south-eastern Cape. They have long, tapering leaves and yellow to reddish flowers, which are sometimes scented. Summer growers, very suitable for planting out during the warmer months.

Cultivation Average shrubby mesem, ie, droughtland treatment.
Propagation Seed or cuttings.

BIJLIA *(Mesembryanthemaceae)*

One species only, *B. cana,* from the Great Karoo. Highly succulent and somewhat resembling a pleiospilos species, with yellow winter flowers.

Cultivation Semi-desert mesem.
Propagation Seed.

BOMBAX *(Bombacaceae)*

A small, caudiciform genus, from tropical Africa and Asia. Of interest, chiefly, to specialist growers.

Cultivation As for tropical caudiciforms.
Propagation Seed.

BRACHYSTELMA *(Asclepiadaceae)*

Dwarf African succulents (much like the tuberous ceropegias) which grow annual stems, with small leaves and dainty flowers. There are few species in collections as yet; but many more are known, which one hopes will soon grace our greenhouses.

Cultivation As for similar African ceropegias.
Propagation Seed. Vine cuttings may root.

BROMELIADS *(Bromeliaceae)*

Most plants belonging to this large group do not properly belong in this volume, even though there are botanists who consider them to be succulents of a special kind. For the most part, however, Bromeliads constitute a different group of plants as far as greenhouse gardening is concerned and this is particularly true of the non-terrestrial kinds.

What will be found in succulent collections are specimens of such terrestrial plants as those belonging to *Abromeitiella* (which has its own entry), *Dyckia, Hechtia, Puya* and one or two other genera. These make handsome additions to any collection and they are often offered in the succulent plant trade.

Cultivation Droughtland to semi-desert. Most species are fairly hardy and simple to grow. Some produce showy flowers.
Propagation Easy from seed, offset cuttings or divisions.

BRYOPHYLLUM *(Crassulaceae)*
It is usual, now, to find the species which were once assigned to this genus listed under *Kalanchoe (qv)*. They are generally the species which produce plantlets on the edges of their leaves.

BURSERA *(Burseraceae)*
Of this large genus of caudiciform xerophytic shrubs from North America, one species only, B. *microphylla,* is usually seen in cultivation. Apart from its grotesque body, which is not without appeal, this species is most notable among caudiciforms for its compound pinnate leaves.

Cultivation Droughtland caudiciform.
Propagation Easy from seed.

CALANDRINIA *(Portulacaceae)*
Not often seen in succulent collections and usually more favoured by alpine plant enthusiasts. However, some species are succulent and others more or less so. Most are very hardy and well worth trying where space is available. Seed is often available from specialist seedsmen.

Cultivation Usually easy. Simple droughtland.
Propagation Seed or cuttings.

CALIBANUS *(Agavaceae)*
The single species, C. *hookeri,* comes from Tamaulipas, Mexico. It grows as a lumpy and eventually a large caudex, attractively covered in curly bark and displaying a number of grasslike tufts of long, blue-green, sharp-edged leaves. Even among caudiciform succulents this is an oddity, although a most attractive one.

Cultivation Simple droughtland caudiciform.
Propagation Seed. Caudexes will grow faster if not raised above the compost for a year or two.

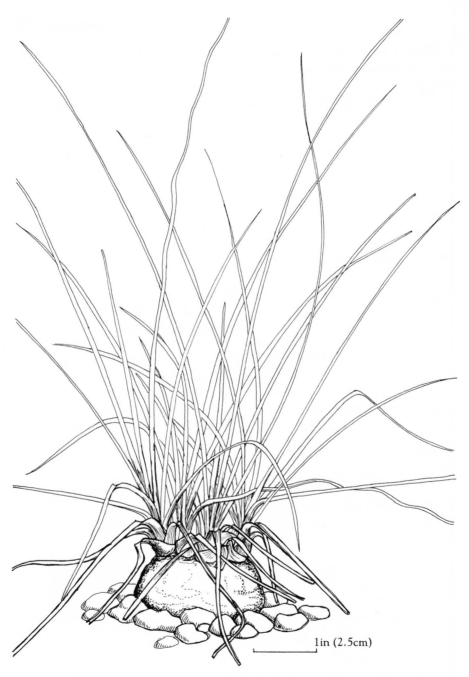

1in (2.5cm)

Calibanus hookeri, a Mexican caudiciform with a handsome, corky body, which increases slowly in size if the plant is confined to a pot. In its nocturnal habitat the species reaches a huge size; the plantsman who re-discovered it refers to one 'as big as a Volkswagen'.

CARALLUMA *(Asclepiadaceae)*
A large genus of stapelia-like succulents, which are widespread on the African continent, with species found as far apart as India and the Canary Islands. Much revision of the genus has already been carried out and is continuing; some species may now be found classified under *Orbea*, *Orbeopsis*, *Tridentea* and other names. To the grower these plants offer a range of fascinating and sometimes infuriating plants, with beautiful flowers.

Cultivation See the special section on stapeliads.
Propagation Seed, cuttings, layerings. Difficult species are, occasionally, grafted on to easier, more vigorous ones.

CARPOBROTUS *(Mesembryanthemaceae)*
Vigorous creeping mat-formers, principally from the Cape Province, with three-angled pointed leaves, yellow or purple flowers and large fruits which in some species are edible. *C. edulis* is the 'Hottentot Fig', unfortunately too large and too fast growing for most pot cultivation. In some warm parts of the British Isles the species has become naturalised and, each year, makes brilliant sheets of colour on cliffs and coastal slopes. Well worth a place in the garden, or its own large container, where either method of growing it is possible. Other species are more modest in their demands.

Cultivation Easy droughtland.
Propagation Seed or cuttings.

CARRUANTHUS *(Mesembryanthemaceae)*
Small clumping mesems, similar to *Faucaria*, with solitary yellow flowers.

Cultivation Easy droughtland.
Propagation Seed or cuttings.

CEPHALOCEREUS *(Cactaceae)*
A largish genus of Central American cacti, mostly columnar in habit and usually possessing a covering of fine spines of hair, especially at the top of the stem. They are easy to grow and they will eventually provide noble specimens for the back of the bench. *C. senilis,* the popular 'Old Man Cactus', a slow growing species from Mexico, is the best known to

cultivation. It is almost always unbranched and covered with long, white hair. Other species are equally deserving of attention, even if flowering is not likely to occur with any of them until they reach a great age.

Cultivation Droughtland to semi-desert. These are easy plants in good light, which will keep the spines or hair in good colour.
Propagation Seed. Beheaded plants will usually branch and provide cutting material when they do. Top cuttings will root, once dried or sealed.

CEPHALOPHYLLUM (*Mesembryanthemaceae*)
A large genus of easily grown, mostly prostrate mesems from the coastal areas of western South Africa. Not as common as they deserve to be, they should at least be sampled by all mesem growers, now that seed of so many species is available. Flowers in many different colours are produced, even on young plants, and may be as large as 4in (10cm) in diameter in some sorts.

Cultivation Droughtland. These are plants which grow and flower during the winter months when they have the choice, and very good light (natural light augmented by artificial lighting) may be necessary to bring some shy species into bloom. Otherwise, cephalophyllums are easy to look after.
Propagation Seed, cuttings or natural layerings.

CERARIA (*Portulacaceae*)
In South Africa and Namibia the members of this small genus may grow into tall shrubs. In cultivation they are nearly always seen as small bonsai-like specimens of considerable appeal, when they can be obtained. Cerarias rarely flower in cultivation but they are worth effort for their very individual appearance.

Cultivation Not too difficult with semi-desert treatment and allowed to follow their own preference for winter growing.
Propagation Not easy. Seed is seldom available and cuttings do not seem to root with much enthusiasm.

CEREUS (*Cactaceae*)
This is now a genus of some twenty to thirty species – many others which were once so called having been split off into a number of other genera,

most of which still retain the older name as a suffix (eg *Pachycereus, Echinocereus,* etc). Cereus species are columnar and usually erect cacti, though some are shrubby and some sprawling. They may grow to a considerable height in nature, as some will in collections, when planted out in beds in large greenhouses. Grown with this amount of space and root run some will produce their beautiful large trumpet flowers. In pots, cereus species are best regarded as non-flowering, but no less worthy on that account.

Cultivation Easy semi-desert.
Propagation Seed or cuttings.

CEROCHLAMYS *(Mesembryanthemaceae)*

A monotypic genus from the Little Karoo. *C. pachyphylla* is stemless and its fleshy leaves have a waxy covering, these colouring well in warm summer sunshine. Flowers of pink to purple grow on short pedicels.

Cultivation Droughtland.
Propagation Seed, cuttings are possible.

CEROPEGIA *(Asclepiadaceae)*

Until fairly recently only a few members of this exciting genus were ever seen in collections. Now, thanks to the enterprise of a growing band of enthusiasts, forty or fifty species are to be found. This leaves perhaps as many as one hundred more to be introduced to cultivation and, almost certainly, new species to be discovered.

Ceropegias occur in many parts of the tropical and subtropical world, principally in forest areas. Southern Africa has given us (so far) over sixty species; more are native to warmer parts of Europe. The Canary Islands and eastern India own more and Madagascar (Malagasy Republic) has its own individual complement. Most species are vining and some have caudexes or tuberous roots. Some are stem succulents, those from the Canary Islands growing as upright bushes with bare stems and being known to growers as 'stick' ceropegias. While it is true that the bare, leafless stems of many of the vines do not have either a very great or a very varied appeal, the marvellous flytrap flowers more than compensate. These are borne in abundance on most mature specimens and are followed, when pollinated, by typical, paired, asclepiad follicles. In colour they display almost every possible colour or combination of colour

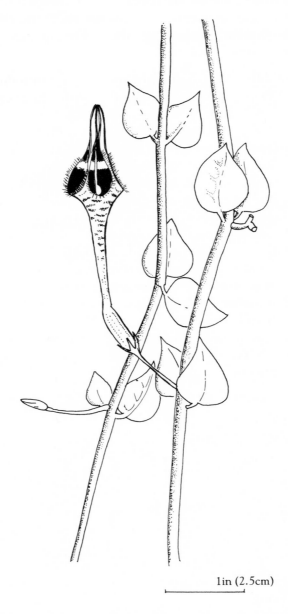

1in (2.5cm)

Ceropegia radicans comes from the Cape Province and grows among scrub bush, its creeping stems rooting at the nodes. The roots are fleshy and the stems sparingly branched, with thick, succulent leaves. The flowers are pale, yellowish-green, with purple dots and flecks, and dark purple-brown within the interior. C. *radicans* makes a fine hanging plant.

and often show shades which are uncommon to most other flowering plants – browns, greens and other rare colours being found. They are quite unlike the flowers produced by other succulents, even those of other asclepiads.

Cultivation Not difficult for most of the species so far introduced. Most are scramblers or twiners in the wild, using the surrounding vegetation in their dry open forest habitats as support. (In cultivation they seem contented either to hang or be trained upwards, according to the wish of their growers.) The 'stick' species are found in littoral situations in the Canary Islands, and should be given brighter conditions and treated as winter growers. Species from Madagascar are less difficult than once supposed (see the note on Madagascan species elsewhere). All ceropegias seem to like water and to appeal to mealy bugs. Spraying with water or a dilute feed will satisfy the first requirement and an occasional misting with a suitable systemic insecticide will deal with the bugs. Like all asclepiads, ceropegias may suddenly rot through at their bases. They are not, however, half as prone to this annoying habit as are some other genera, and good drainage at their necks plus bottom watering for the more delicate species should prevent it.

Propagation Easy from seed or from cuttings. Almost any section of a healthy vine, which has several nodes, should root with reasonable ease, sometimes from each node.

CHAMAECEREUS (*Cactaceae*)

This once monotypic genus has been sunk without trace into *Lobivia* or *Echinopsis*, by unfeeling non gardening botanists. However, *Chamaecereus sylvestrii*, the 'Peanut Cactus' deserves to keep its name, if only as a reward for its long years of service to our hobby. There are now several forms plus numerous named hybrids between the species and other suitable cacti which have given us a range of colours to add to its original flame-coloured blooms. Hybridisation has also produced plants with an attractive variety of spines and forms, and if none surpasses the old freely flowering favourites, that could not be expected. Most of them are, at least, worth growing.

Cultivation As for droughtland cacti, but more shade and moisture are preferable.

Propagation Whole stem cuttings or seed.

CHEIRIDOPSIS (Mesembryanthemaceae)

This is a large genus, with great diversity of form and leaf shape among its hundreds or so species. Cheiridopsis are winter growers, from the western side of the Cape and reaching up as far as Namibia. They are indispensable for brightening the greenhouse with their flowers (usually white or yellow) during the dull weeks which sometimes seem to stretch endlessly out between Christmas and spring. The difference in appearance between the green specimens which are the result of poor light and the beautiful, almost white or silvery grey ones, which have been fortunate in their owners can be almost unbelievable. Very good light is also essential for good flowering.

Cultivation As for winter growing, desert succulents, with very good light. High temperatures do not seem to be necessary and, like their kind, these plants are fairly hardy.

Propagation Usually from seed, which soon gives flowering size plants. Cuttings are also easy to root.

CISSUS (Vitaceae)

This name is now properly reserved for those plants which have a climbing habit. The caudiciform species which do not make vining growth are now classified as *Cyphostemma* and will be found under that name. What are now regarded as *Cissus* species are a widespread, tropical race of attractive climbers, which cling by tendrils and which produce small bisexual flowers in cymes, followed by berries. Some species are particularly attractive, but all seem to prefer warm moist conditions.

Cultivation Warm moist forest treatment – given this, cissus species might make good indoor plants.

Propagation Seed if available, or cuttings of at least one joint.

CLEISTOCACTUS (Cactaceae)

Best known for the lovely white-spined *Cleistocactus strausii*, this easily grown genus of South American columnar cacti has other attractive members worth their space on the bench. These are branching plants, which eventually make fine mature specimens in large pots. Some, when old enough, will produce their vivid tubular flowers.

Cultivation Ordinary semi-desert treatment.

Propagation Easy from seed. Stems may be beheaded, which encourages branching, and the top cutting rooted after drying or sealing.

COLEUS (Labiatae)

Not many labiates are found in succulent plant collections. In this large genus there are several species which, if barely succulent, fit in well and are sometimes grown. They certainly deserve a place. Apart from their attractiveness, they bring blue flowers, a rare colour among succulents, and intensely aromatic foliage, which is also unusual.

Cultivation Simple forest treatment, not too moist, nor too dry, although a bright position keeps the growth tight. Like the non-succulent species the xerophytic ones make good house plants.
Propagation Usually from cuttings, although seed is also possible.

CONOPHYTUM (Mesembryanthemaceae)

This very large genus of 'mimicry' plants is next in popularity to the lithops and, now that many more species are coming into cultivation, more and more mesem collectors are being attracted to them. Conophytums are very varied in form and flower and also in the colour of their bodies and blooms, the latter being white, yellow, pink or purple, in many shades. When grown well, these charming, miniature, desert mesems soon make tight clumps, every head of which should flower regularly.

Cultivation These are winter growing, desert plants. They are very hardy, but should not be allowed to get too cold during winter so that watering (with care) may continue. The beginning of the growing season is usually indicated by flower buds pushing their way through the split, dead skin of the previous year's growth. At this stage just a little water may be given and the amount increased as the new bodies plump up and the flower buds enlarge towards flowering. After the flowers die, regular watering should be discontinued and the plants allowed to dry almost completely and remain so, under their dry skins until the next season begins, in late summer. Very bright light is essential for most species and excellent drainage. The compost for conophytums should not contain much humus, although, when active, they will appreciate reasonable feeding.
Propagation Seed or cuttings.

COPIAPOA (Cactaceae)

Small, globular, terrestrial cacti from the dry north of Chile. Some species have brown or dark-grey bodies and some are covered in a chalky white wax. All flowers are yellow and produced in the woolly crown of the plant.

Cultivation As for desert cacti. Over-watering must be guarded against at all times.
Propagation Not difficult from seed.

CORRYOCACTUS (Cactaceae)

A small genus of Andean cacti, which grow as branched shrubby plants in nature. The flowers are red or yellow.

Cultivation Semi-desert to desert treatment.
Propagation Seed or cuttings. Young plants have attractively coloured spination.

CORYPHANTHA (Cactaceae)

Terrestrial cacti from Mexico and the American Southwest. Close to the genus *Mammillaria,* they should be grown as such. The flowers are almost always yellow and produced from near the crown of the plants.

Cultivation Generally easy, as for other droughtland cacti. Some species, however, originate in true desert areas, and these need less water and more care.
Propagation Seed or sometimes offsets.

COTYLEDON (Crassulaceae)

A genus of shrubby or semi-shrubby succulents, principally from South Africa. Most form clumps and, in time, bear terminal inflorescences of hanging red or yellow bells, which are very showy in the larger species. At their best, which is not hard to achieve for them, these are lovely, even spectactular, plants.

Opuntia phaeacantha. The various forms of this sprawling, clumping cactus are among the commonest prickly pears of the American Southwest. Mature specimens in cultivation will produce flowers and fruit fairly readily

Cultivation Not difficult. Semi-desert treatment is suitable. Very good light is always necessary for the larger species, especially for the white, farinose forms of *Cotyledon orbiculata*. These plants are winter growers (although some activity may be noticed at other times) and they usually flower in spring. Spraying the white forms can badly mark the leaves and rosette centres rot easily if water is allowed to remain in them.
Propagation Easy from seed or leaf and stem cuttings.

CRASSULA (*Crassulaceae*)

It is frequently one of the species in this genus which brings another new-comer into the succulent plant hobby, and for this reason crassulas are sometimes dismissed as beginners' plants. Fortunately there are enough real gardeners to ignore such superior opinions and keep the plants themselves where they should be, at the very front of things succulent.

Crassulas form a very large genus, and not all of them are succulent – some species are even aquatic. The succulent species are, for the most part, natives of South Africa, with several species in tropical Africa and others stationed further afield.

For gardening purposes the genus may conveniently be considered in terms of its extremes. There are the tallish (to 3ft [1m]) arborescent species, of which *Crassula ovata* (sometimes listed or sold as *C. argentea* or *C. portulacea*) is typical. The species forms a thick-stemmed and much-branched shrub, with fleshy leaves which fall from the older stems as they age. Its habitat is on slopes or rock outcrops, often in association with scrub vegetation, usually in sheltered situations and sometimes shaded by tree growth. *C. ovata* comes from the eastern side of South Africa, where the soil is good and there is abundant summer rain.

In complete contrast, *C. alstonii* comes from a much less hospitable part of the African continent, northern Namaqualand, on the western side – an extremely dry area with great heat in summer and occasional winter rains. It is the habitat of such extreme succulents as the dwarf mesems (in particular conophytums), and *C. alstonii*, a beautiful little crassula, is also greatly modified to cope with its environment. The species is small and whitish green, with its leaves closely pressed against

Ceropegia haygarthii 'Yellow Form' is a variation which has flowers of diluted colour. All the members of the genus have similarly unusual blooms, which are often followed by paired seed horns

each other in an overlapping fashion and tightly clasping the stem.

In between these two very different species, from opposite sides of southern Africa, are ranged a number of other crassulas, perhaps as many as two hundred, including the hybrid forms. Their variety of shape and colour is unparalleled elsewhere in the succulent plant kingdom, except perhaps for the euphorbias. Most are easy to grow and will flower regularly; there are always species showing blooms, at every time of year.

Cultivation This will vary from dry forest treatment for the shrubby and tree-like species to desert treatment for the tiny 'mimicry' types, which, it should be remembered, are winter growers. Most species will respond well to droughtland cultivation, only the highly adapted species being at all fussy.

Propagation Very easy for most species, either from seed or cuttings, leaf or stem.

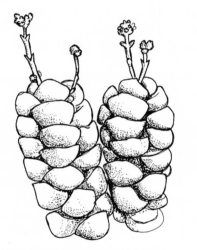

1in (2.5cm)

Crassula alstonii belongs to the *Sphaerica* section of the genus and comes from northern Namaqualand. Desert treatment is necessary to prevent growth from becoming too loose and the colour too green. The tiny flowers are white and appear during winter.

CRYPTOCEREUS (*Cactaceae*)

Epiphytic cacti, vigorous in growth, with attractive nocturnal fragrant flowers. The stems are rich green in colour and deeply lobed, which gives the plants the popular name of 'Rick-rack Cacti'.

Cultivation As for other jungle cacti.
Propagation Seed or cuttings.

CYNANCHUM *(Asclepiadaceae)*

A large tropical and subtropical genus, from which a number of succulent-stemmed species are now coming into the collections of discerning growers. These are all scramblers or climbers which produce tiny flowers in abundance, sometimes fragrant and always beautiful. Though at first appreciated for their blooms, it is now being realised that in some species the rough and irregular stems also have their appeal.

Cultivation Dry to wet forest.
Propagation Seed or cuttings.

CYPHOSTEMMA *(Vitaceae)*

These were once included in *Cissus*. They are caudiciform succulents, the caudexes of which may become extremely large after many years in optimum conditions. In pots they will not outgrow their welcome, crowning their trunks with seasonal fresh green leaves which sometimes open in delightful shades of red or copper, as do some poplar trees. On mature specimens small flowers are followed by red or yellow fruits.

Cultivation Droughtland caudiciform.
Propagation Seed.

DECARYIA *(Didiereaceae)*

Decaryia madagascariensis is the single species in the genus. A tree in habitat, it grows much less vigorously in a pot, becoming no more than a dense, xerophytic shrub whose branches present an odd, zigzaggy appearance, with small leaves and pairs of spines at each angle.

Cultivation As for other Madagascan, dry forest endemics. Not too cold at any time.
Propagation From cuttings, which are slow to root, or seed, if ever available.

DELOSPERMA *(Mesembryanthemaceae)*

A large genus of well over one hundred species of small or dwarf bushy shrubs, with a wide distribution in southern Africa. Most species soon make attractive, free flowering specimens, whose blooms may be white, yellow, red or purple and which do not open until noon.

Cultivation Easy droughtland. Delosperma make excellent garden plants, in a dry sunny position, but are not quite hardy enough to be left outside permanently, though the harder-leaved species may persist for a year or two.

Propagation Simple, from either seed or cuttings. Many species are now available from specialist seedsmen.

DIDIEREA *(Didiereaceae)*

This is a very small genus of Madagascan trees with succulent stems. They are often likened to cacti. They are not easy to obtain, nor to keep successfully in cultivation for very long. Nevertheless, nursery-grown specimens are obtainable from overseas at a price. One wishes that they were easier to care for and, therefore, seen more often. There is nothing quite like them.

Cultivation As for other Madagascan dry forest xerophytes. These plants will grow for most of the year, but should have an almost dry period allowed, once the leaves fall. Warmth is needed at all times.

Propagation Seed or cuttings, if available. Neither method is easy.

DINTERANTHUS *(Mesembryanthemaceae)*

Native to hot dry areas in Namibia, and usually found growing in quartz fields, this genus is very close, botanically to *Lithops,* with which it has been hybridised. These are really beautiful little plants, which are not too difficult to grow. Golden flowers may be expected from late summer onward.

Cultivation As for *Lithops* or *Conophytum.* Only enough water should be given to prevent plant bodies from dulling in appearance and wrinkling. Even a small excess of water will almost certainly cause the body to split, which may not be fatal to the plant, but will spoil its appearance for a whole year. Very good light is essential, to bring out the real beauty of these dwarf mesems. At their best they resemble semi-precious stones.

Propagation Seed, which is dustlike and which should not be buried. These seeds prefer to germinate in the light. Not difficult if care is taken.

DIOSCOREA *(Dioscoreaceae)*

Out of a huge genus of more than five hundred species (which include the yam) several are prized in succulent plant collections, though only one is commonly seen. *D. elephantipes,* the one species which is still often called by its older name of *Testudinaria elephantipes* may, without much argument, be considered the most extraordinary caudiciform of all those now grown. The toughly spherical caudex, whose brown, corky bark divides and redivides as it increases in size resembles little else among succulent plants. The speed with which the annual vine grows when it is once started into life often astonishes those people who think of succulents as slow growing plants. Other species are worth trying, but are less striking in appearance and less reliable.

Cultivation Easy. Dormancy and growth will show themselves as the plant itself decides (see the section on caudiciform succulents). Once the vining stem or stems appear, watering may be generous and feeding is essential. Do not let the caudex dry right out during the rest period.
Propagation Seed. Patience is needed if large caudexes are to be expected but they will eventually grow into what is wanted.

DIPLOCYATHA *(Asclepiadaceae)*
Now included in *Orbea* by some botanists, *D. ciliata* has very individual flowers and prominent long white hairs on the edges of its lobes, which move constantly in the slightest breeze. The blooms are almost white, roughly papillose and free of any stapeliad smell, the plant itself growing as a small clump of four-angled toothed stems.

Cultivation Usual stapeliad, with care in watering.
Propagation Seed or stem cuttings.

DISCHIDIA *(Asclepiadaceae)*
Many of these epiphytic, tropical, trailing plants are known; but few are seen in collections, except for the handful which are valued in specialist, asclepiad greenhouses. Some species have their leaves modified into water retaining pitchers. The flowers are tiny, usually white, yellow or red, with very constricted mouths to their tubes.

Cultivation As for jungle, or rain-forest succulents, but never too cold. The treatment which suits hoyas should content them. Dischidias are worth more attention; their foliage is varied and attractive and their flowering, when abundant, adds to their charm.
Propagation Usually from cuttings, although seed is possible.

DOROTHEANTHUS *(Mesembryanthemaceae)*

This is a small genus of annual carpeters, from the Cape and Namaqualand, usually grown as garden hybrids, the popular 'Livingstone Daisies'. The species are dainty and colourful, if non-perennial plants are not looked upon with too much disfavour.

Cultivation Simple mesem.
Propagation Seed.

DORSTENIA *(Moraceae)*

This is a large genus of tropical rain-forest plants, principally from the eastern side of the African continent. Few species are succulent, but they are all of interest, especially so because of their remarkable inflorescences. These take the form of a flattish head, surrounded by narrow bracks, the head composed of a number of small flowers which together appear to be one large one. Single seeds are ejected to some distance by an explosive mechanism. If only one species can be grown, this should be *D. foetida,* because of its attractive caudex and its free flowering.

Cultivation Easy if given moist, warm conditions and allowed to grow for most, if not all, of the year.
Propagation Cuttings, or seed, which sometimes sets itself near the parent plant.

DROSANTHEMUM *(Mesembryanthemaceae)*

Considering the size of the genus and the availability of seed of so many species, it is odd that these plants are not more often cultivated. The foliage is varied and leaves have tiny papillae on their surfaces, which glisten in the sun. Flowering is abundant and the blooms come in many colours, opening in the afternoon. Drosanthemums do well in the garden during the summer and should be kept in a bright situation, under glass, in winter.

Cultivation As for other shrubby mesems.
Propagation Cuttings or seed. Seedlings often flower in their first year.

DUDLEYA *(Crassulaceae)*

A genus of handsome, rosette plants, comprising nearly fifty species and forms, from Mexico and the American Southwest. Close to the echeverias from which they differ in some floral characteristics, their own flowers are showy and brighten the greenhouse in spring with their colourful red, orange, yellow or white. Dudleyas are typically thought of as extremely farinose, snow-white succulents, but there are equally attractive species in the genus which have bright-green or pearly-grey leaves.

Cultivation Easy droughtland. Dudleyas should be allowed to remain active in winter, to prepare for flowering. Spraying dislodges the plentiful powder of the white species, but does not damage the appearance of the foliage. Dudleyas seem to like elongating their stems, so that their rosettes eventually hang as a curtain. If this habit is not admired, or is found inconvenient, rosettes may be cut off and rooted. Leaves do not appear to root, as one might expect in these members of the Crassulaceae.
Propagation Rosette cuttings. Plants which have been beheaded should be stood in the shade and sprayed well, to encourage shooting. Seed is

1in (2.5cm)

Dudleya traskeae (ISI 962), one of the white dudleyas, with leaves which are thickly covered with farina. The species is now very rare, possibly extinct in its one station, Santa Barbara Island, off the Californian coast. The illustration is of a plant which was grown from a rooted cutting distributed by the International Succulent Institute. By supporting such organisations, even the amateur grower can help the conservation movement.

often produced in quantity and chance seedlings sometimes spring up around the parent plant or in nearby pots. However, in view of the promiscuous nature of dudleyas, any progeny should be considered to be hybrids. Crosses with other members of the Crassulaceae are not impossible.

DUVALIA (Asclepiadaceae)
A small genus of low growing, clumping, stapeliads, from various regions in South Africa and Namibia, East Africa and arabia. The flowers are tiny, but distinctive, especially those which are chocolate brown. all have a prominent raised centre and some species have their lobes fringed with cilia.

Cultivation Droughtland. Most species grow in the shade of other vegetation. In the greenhouse they frequently do best if planted in the grit at the base of a 'tree' crassula or similar form of larger plant. As stapeliads go, duvalias are easy to grow, but drainage must always be excellent.
Propagation Seed, which is usually obtainable for most species. It should always be set on edge and may germinate exceedingly quickly. Cuttings of stem sections are easy to root and clumps may often be divided into ready rooted pieces.

EBERLANZIA (Mesembryanthemaceae)
A small genus of shrubby mesems, from the Cape Province and elsewhere, notable for the possession of twiggy thorns which derive from old inflorescences or from sterile flower stalks. In habitat most species grow as well-armoured thorny hummocks, under which protection a miniature ecosystem of tiny plants and insect life pursues its unnoticed existence. Eberlanzias have papillose leaves and pink to purplish flowers.

Cultivation As for other easy, shrubby mesems.
Propagation Seed. Cuttings might also be possible.

EBRACTEOLA (Mesembryanthemaceae)
A little known genus in cultivation, but those species whose seed has become available have proved to be delightful miniatures, with pink or white flowers, which almost hide the plant, in due season.

Cultivation Simple mesem.

Propagation Seed or cuttings. Seedlings soon make neat clumps of linear, green leaves, which grow in rosettes upon a much thickened, caudex-like rootstock.

ECHEVERIA (*Crassulaceae*)

This large genus and its many hybrids combine to provide many of the glories of the succulent plant world. Unfortunately, there is a macho element on the spinier side of the hobby, which sometimes dismisses the echeveria group as 'women's plant'. This opinion says much for the excellent taste of lady growers and should firmly recommend these plants to all lovers of beautiful things.

Echeverias are chiefly native in Mexico, with species found in Central and South America as well as in the United States. Their habitats are very varied; they are found at many altitudes and in several types of country, open, woodland or even on exposed cliff faces. In cultivation they seem to prefer to grow all the year round and one or more sorts will be flowering in a collection at any time of year, although the main season is in early spring.

Echeverias are rosette plants, some stemless, some erect and branching. The stemless species increase themselves by division, by producing offsets, or by building themselves into mounds or clumps. Some species trail on elongated stems, some grow upwards, the main stem hardening into a trunk and then branching, until a tree-like form is achieved, with rosettes at the ends of the branches. All species, and their hybrids, begin to produce their beautiful, bell flowers when quite young, in shades of red, orange, pink or yellow, or a combination of these colours. As for the plants themselves, their leaves display almost every available shade and colour, from silver or near white to a deep brown or purple which is almost black. In addition, they may be smooth or rough, silky or bristly and frosted or powdery, and such is the range of colour and texture that colour displays and effects may be created to rival anything in the garden.

Cultivation The section on rosette succulents should be consulted. Most echeverias and hybrids will give little trouble. One point is important, however; no group of plants is so likely to reward over-generous treatment and poor light with such green, bloated plants. Compost for all of them should be gritty and on the poor side, with reasonable feeding and no more. Only a spartan diet will produce really good specimens.

Propagation Most of these plants will root easily from leaves, although rosette cuttings will produce new plants more quickly and are sometimes necessary in the case of the thinner-leaved sorts. Beheading a specimen which has grown too tall or top heavy will usually free new growths from the truncated stem, especially if this is placed in the shade and sprayed. Seed is also possible.

ECHIDNOPSIS (*Asclepiadaceae*)

A small genus of more or less prostrate plants with intricately branched sinuous stems which have a tesselated appearance and more ribs than most other stapeliads. The flowers are tiny and carried at the end of the stems. Coming from the warmer parts of South Africa, Arabia and tropical Africa these very individual stapeliads like warmth in cultivation.

Cultivation As for other stapeliads.
Propagation Whole, side stem cuttings, which often detach themselves and root down into the compost.

ECHINOCACTUS (*Cactaceae*)

This was formerly the name used for a whole group of cacti, but now reserved for one genus. The species vary; some are large and solitary, others smaller and clustering. Flowers are produced in the woolly crown of the plant; they are bell-shaped, occasionally red, but usually yellow. This genus is best known for E. *grusonii,* the 'Golden Barrel', a favourite exhibitor's plant, once it has reached the large size needed for possible success.

Cultivation As for other semi-desert, terrestrial cacti from Mexico.
Propagation Seed or offsets, when these are available.

ECHINOCEREUS (*Cactaceae*)

This is a large, varied and very hardy genus of cacti, from Mexico and the south-western United States, with some species found further north. They are either solitary or clumping plants, according to the species, and many will flower regularly once they are adult, which may be in as short a time as two years from seed. Echinocereus species are, in general, easy to grow and flower, the blooms of some being large and showy, in pink, green, red or purple, with bright stigma lobes. Some species are slightly scented.

Cultivation Semi-desert cactus. Little or no heat is needed under glass.
Propagation Best from seed, although stem cuttings will usually root.

ECHINOFOSSULOCACTUS (*Cactaceae*)
Sometimes called *Stenocactus* (especially on small labels) this is an easily
grown genus of Mexican, globular cacti, distinctive because of their thin
ribs and widely spaced areoles, the ribs wavy and numerous in almost
every species. The flowers are small, but attractive, and are usually yellowish, pink or white, the petals often marked with a contrasting,
median line.

Cultivation Semi-desert.
Propagation Easy from seed.

ECHINOPSIS (*Cactaceae*)
The genus *Echinopsis* should now be taken to include such well known,
older names as *Pseudolobivia*, *Trichocereus*, *Helianthocereus* and others, a
re-classification which does not help growers much. Those looking for
what was once the sort of cactus usually implied by the generic name (a
fast growing globular plant, not always of much interest in itself, but
freely flowering and producing very large nocturnal blooms, often beautifully scented) should choose from among what are sometimes called the
'true' echinopsis forms: *E. eyriesii*, *E. hamatacantha*, *E. multiplex* and
others, including hybrids.

Cultivation Easy droughtland, with some shade.
Propagation Seed or offsets. Stem cuttings of columnar sorts.

EDITHCOLEA (*Asclepiadaceae*)
One species only, *E. grandis*, exists, which is close to the carallumas and
difficult to grow, or at least to maintain for very long. The flowers are
showy and large.

Cultivation As for other stapeliads, but skill and care are needed, even
more than usual.
Propagation Seed, which is often obtainable. Seedlings grow well
enough and may even flower before the plant's inevitable demise. However, it is often possible to salvage good cuttings from the wreck and
these root fairly easily in warm conditions.

ENDADENIUM *(Euphorbiaceae)*
Very close to *Euphorbia* *(qv)*.

EPICACTUS *(Cactaceae)*
This is a term used to cover a wide variety of hybrid cacti, derived from epiphytic, jungle species and crosses. Most have very showy flowers, which are an improvement upon those of their ancestors, at least in one respect; they remain open during the day.

EPIPHYLLANTHUS *(Cactaceae)*
This is a small genus, now included in *Schlumbergera*. The name is included here as the species which comprised it are often so listed. These small epiphytes are not always easy to please and will sometimes collapse into a pile of stem sections, just when things appear to be going well. Nevertheless, they are pleasing miniatures, with lovely flowers and are worth the effort to grow well.

Cultivation As for rain forest epiphytes, with more care than the larger, vigorous kinds need. Epiphyllanthus should never be allowed to become too wet or too dry, nor should their compost be allowed to compact itself. Spraying is often safer than watering, as long as the soil is not dry.
Propagation Seed or cuttings. If plant collapse occurs much of its remains will root; some stem pieces will be already rooted.

EPIPHYLLUM *(Cactaceae)*
A small genus of epiphytic cacti, usually with long, flat leaf-like joints, aerial roots and seldom spined. The species are not much cultivated, although they deserve to be; the genus is best known for the many intergeneric hybrids which now exist. Breeders have produced these with huge blooms, in many bright colours, which are freely produced and which stay open during the daytime. They have become extremely popular, particularly with gardeners who do not consider the graceful, nocturnal flowers of the species sufficient reward for their labours.

Cultivation See Epiphyllanthus.
Propagation Seed or cuttings.

EREPSIA *(Mesembryanthemaceae)*
Shrubby mesems, with glabrous foliage and pretty flowers, which are

usually white or purple. They are good for planting out in the garden during summer.

Cultivation Easy mesem.
Propagation Seed or cuttings.

ESCOBARIA *(Cactaceae)*

There has been and still is much botanical argument over this genus. Other genera, such as *Cochiseia, Ortegocactus, Neobesseya* and even more may be found under its name, which is retained here as it is still in both amateur and commercial use. In general terms, these are small, globular cacti from Mexico and the American Southwest, with pale-coloured flowers, borne near the top of the plant. Whatever their name should be, the cacti in this group are beautiful and not very difficult to grow and flower.

Cultivation As for other semi-desert cacti.
Propagation Seed or occasionally, offsets.

ESPOSTOA *(Cactaceae)*

A small genus of very beautiful South American columnar cacti. They are much prized by collectors for the covering of dense, long hair, often snow white in colour, which completely envelops the stems. Even as small seedlings these plants begin to display their charms, and at least one or two species should be in every, general, succulent collection.

Cultivation Easy enough if treated as typical droughtland or semi-desert cacti.
Propagation Seed. Stem cuttings will root.

EUPHORBIA *(Euphorbiaceae)*

Of this huge genus, the succulent species alone number several hundred, with almost certainly more to be discovered. Most succulent euphorbias are native to the African continent and its neighbouring islands; India and Sri Lanka have their own complement and there are a few American species. In all, euphorbias offer the collector a remarkably diverse choice of succulents and xerophytes. This includes a number of richly varied species in which some have, because of convergent evolution, 'mimicked' other succulents. Such names as *Euphorbia opuntioides* and others illustrate this tendency very well.

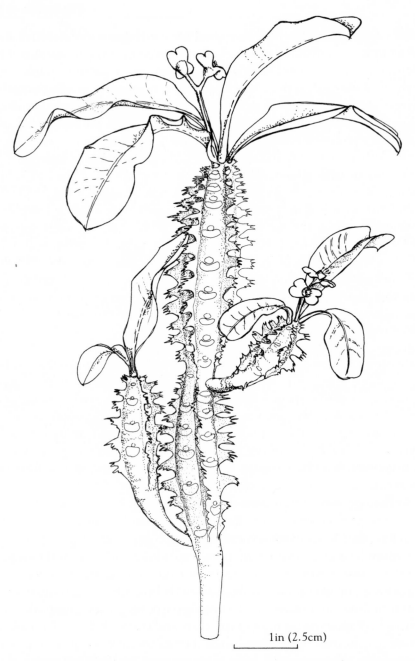

1in (2.5cm)

Euphorbia lophogona, from Madagascar. It needs warmth and humidity, but is otherwise easy to grow. In cultivation it will eventually reach 2ft (50cm) in height. The leathery leaves are dark green and the constantly recurring flowers white to pale-pink.

All euphorbias are linked by a similarity of inflorescence. This takes the form of a cyathium, in which the flowers are tiny and reduced to essentials, and surrounded by bracts, which are sometimes large and brightly coloured. It is these bracts which are frequently referred to as the 'flowers' of euphorbias, by growers and which often give them their colourful appeal as 'flowering' plants. The 'Crown of Thorns' group and the florist's poinsettias are popular examples.

Euphorbias may be found occupying ecological niches in every sort of environment from true desert to rain forest and much of the old disappointment with these fascinating plants has arisen from a failure to realise this fact and to treat most of them as if they were desert cacti. Without knowing the correct name of a euphorbia, so that reference books may be consulted, it is hardly possible to guess at the treatment which it should have. Nevertheless, there are sometimes indications to be found in the form of an unknown plant which may help. It is unfortunate that the lists of seedsmen and plant dealers so often give nothing more than names, with no advice at all as to the cultivation which the plants require.

Cultivation All caudiciform species of *Euphorbia* should have the caudex raised above the compost, when potted up, and be given very good drainage. Similarly, species with a tuberous or napiform root should also have this raised. The medusid types such as *E. caput-medusae* or *E. inermis* are typical. All euphorbias of this sort should be treated with care; less so in the case of the vigorous growers and much more so with such geophytes as *E. hypogaea*, although such species are not likely to come the way of the novice grower.

At the opposite extreme are such leafy species as *E. milii v. splendens*, the 'Crown of Thorns', and many related species, which usually come from Madagascar (Malagasy Republic). Such plants are easy to grow and may often be seen growing well as unlabelled houseplants, in the collections of growers who may not even suspect their succulent nature. In fact, this group of euphorbias should strictly be called xerophytes but the distinction is unimportant for gardening purposes. Forest plants all, they may be kept growing for most of the year, and they will flower over a long period. A shortish 'dry' period should be allowed, perhaps in midsummer, so that leaves may fall and the plants relax and rest. However, they should not dry right out and spraying will keep stem tips green and encourage leafing up after the rest period.

In general, there are many euphorbias which may be grown easily and permanently. It is the author's opinion (shared by other collectors who grow these desirable plants) that much of the trouble experienced over the years has arisen because euphorbias have been under-watered and under-nourished. If allowed to become too dry during their dormant period, especially if this occurs in the warmest season, plants may well shrivel and die back at the tips of their stems, or collapse at ground level because of the weight of the stems. The first complaint has often been diagnosed as red spider and the second as 'rot', whereas it is quite probable that both were due to the lack of food and water.

Euphorbias of the South African semi-deserts and droughtland, such species as *E. pseudocactus, E. grandicornis, E. confinalis* and many more should be grown in the same way as the cacti from similar habitats which they superficially resemble. These euphorbias are usually grown quickly and easily from seed and eventually outgrow their space. However, they are still worth having. When too large they may be cut down to re-shoot, or their cuttings may be rooted after good sealing.

Other species may be tried, on the advice of a good nurseryman. Some guide as to difficulty may be found in the price asked for euphorbias. As a rule, the more expensive they are the less suitable they will be for those growers who are new to the genus.

Propagation This ranges from very simple to very difficult. Economically priced seed, in specialist lists, should soon give attractive plants. Some such as the small popular globular species, eg, *E. obesa*, though not too difficult, are slow growing and should be treated carefully. Cuttings (where possible) should be tried – many will root, even if slowly.

Euphorbias are succulents which sometimes produce their own seed. When ripe it is usually ejected with force, sometimes to a considerable distance, making its recovery unlikely. For this reason various methods of trapping seed have been devised, not all of which are completely satisfactory. Small species can be placed in a small plastic-topped propagator

Stapelianthus madagascariensis belongs to a genus endemic to Madagascar (Malagasy Republic); it is the only stapeliad genus on the island. It needs care in cultivation and should then produce a prostrate mat of tangled stems, on which are displayed the unique rough-surfaced flowers

Titanopsis schwantesii. The generic name refers to the chalky appearance which the tubercled leaves of these plants should possess when grown properly; that is, in as much light as possible, at all times of the year

or stood in an unused fish tank and the exploded seeds picked up as they appear. It is the large specimens which present difficulties, and solutions have been suggested, the favourite one being to cover either the whole plant or the tops of the stem with fine gauze or other material. However, a much simpler technique requires no more complication than the harvesting of the seed before it explodes. As soon as the seed cases begin to turn from green to brown (or to whichever colour accompanies their ripening) one of them should be detached and broken open. In many cases it will be found that the seeds themselves are ripening and are no longer green, even if the cases are. If this is so, all pods should be detached and put into a small glass jar (the lid left a little loose to allow the escape of any moisture) which is then stood in a warm dry place. Eventually the sound of exploding seeds will be heard and once all the pods have shattered the seed should be sown at once. Using this method, germination rates have been extremely high.

The propagation of euphorbias from cuttings has already been discussed in the section on vegetative increase. Here it should be necessary only to stress the importance of not allowing cuttings to lose too much vitality before they are inserted in the propagator, and to remind readers that euphorbia latex can be toxic and extremely irritant. One last note is also of importance. There are a number of euphorbias, the medusids and similar species which present a special problem to propagators. When removed, branches will root fairly easily, but will not form a typical plant with a central body. A method to overcome this disability is now being used with some success. If a branch cutting is taken and rooted it should then be potted up and grown on until properly established. It can then be detached just above the compost level and used as a cutting for the second time, the stump usually forming a typical plant as a result. The technique is a new one and it may have a wide application perhaps even for non-euphorbias.

Epiphyllum 'Cooperi' is an old favourite among the many varieties of orchid cactus which now exist. Its magnificent blooms and heady perfume are still unsurpassed

Euphorbia lophogona comes from one of the wettest parts of Madagascar (Malagasy Republic). In the greenhouse it needs shade, warmth, humidity and good feeding; if these are provided, it should flower for most of the year

Dioscorea elephantipes is perhaps the most bizarre of all the caudiciform succulents. The large corky body stores water for the dry season and when the rains come it grows a mass of leafy vine, with tiny yellowish flowers

FAUCARIA (Mesembryanthemaceae)

Thirty or so species of this popular genus are found in the eastern Cape and the Karoo region. *Faucaria tigrina* is popularly called 'Tiger's Jaws' and the commonest of the other species have similar nicknames, given because the pairs of leaves of these highly adapted, dwarf mesems have conspicuous teeth along their edges. These are easy, beautiful plants, which nearly all have large golden-yellow flowers up to 2½in (6cm) in diameter, and attractively-marked bodies.

Cultivation Dwarf mesem treatment. They are not difficult plants and usually follow British seasons, although they flower late in the year and should be kept growing until the year ends.
Propagation Seed or cutting; both methods are simple.

FENESTRARIA (Mesembryanthemaceae)

'Baby's Toes', *Fenestraria aurantiaca,* is found in the coastal desert areas of Namibia where it grows with its stems completely buried in the sand, exposing only the translucent tips. The flowers are yellow or white and the two species are winter growers. In cultivation *Fenestrarias* species are grown well up out of the compost and are usually given a compost made up of little else but sand or grit. In habitat there is hardly any rain, the plants surviving upon coastal mists and fog.

Cultivation As for the more difficult mesems, with excellent drainage and little water. Spraying is beneficial.
Propagation Seed, although carefully taken cuttings will root.

FEROCACTUS (Cactaceae)

These are 'Barrel' cacti, from Mexico and the American Southwest. Some, after many years, grow very large, in the wild; in cultivation they grow slowly and may be enjoyed for a long time. The spines in this genus are stout and often handsomely recurved, centrals are sometimes deep red and translucent. There are now intergeneric hybrids to be obtained.

Cultivation Not difficult. As for other semi-desert cacti from this part of the world.
Propagation Seed. Seedlings grow slowly, but spines are conspicuous from an early age and young plants most colourful.

FICUS *(Moraceae)*
Out of a very large genus, a very few have adapted to droughtland habitats. Their odd, swollen stems earn them the right to be called caudiciforms, at least in the eyes of some enthusiasts, and *Ficus palmeri* is much prized among collectors who specialise in these plants.

Cultivation Dry forest caudiciform.
Propagation Seed.

FOCKEA *(Asclepiadaceae)*
Stem succulents or xerophytes, with large caudexes, from Angola and the Karoo area. The species are dioecious and produce long annual vining growths, some of which are most attractive. Flowers do not often appear.

Cultivation Not difficult, as for droughtland caudiciforms. Plenty of water may be given when vines are growing and it is best not to allow the caudex to dry right out during the dormant period.
Propagation Seed. Stem cuttings sometimes root.

FOUQUIERIA *(Fouquieriaceae)*
These are native to Mexico, California and Baja California, where the conspicuous, usually red, flowers brighten the landscape. Fouquierias are xerophytic trees and shrubs, rather than succulents in the strict sense. However, all the species make attractive pot specimens, with their strongly spined stems and small, deciduous leaves: some have thickened stems which endear them to caudiciform enthusiasts.

Cultivation Droughtland to semi-desert. Not difficult.
Propagation Cuttings will root but fouquierias are usually grown from seed. Seedlings have a fault, shared by one or two other types of succulent: if disturbed by pricking out or transplanting when young, they may sulk for a while (even as long as several months) before resuming growth. For this reason they are best grown on until they fill their pots and have a good root ball, when they can easily be potted on as a clump into a larger pot.

FRAILEA *(Cactaceae)*
The miniature beauty of these South American cacti gives them enthusiastic admirers among gardeners whose eyes are not caught only by

1in (2.5cm)

the large and impressive. Most fraileas will grow happily in small pots, singly, or as small colonies in 3-4in (7.5-10cm) pots. A mixed collection in a pan would take up little space and allow the contrasting attractions of their bodies and spines to be appreciated. Most species are cleistogamous, and the yellow flowers will open only on bright days, if they are so inclined, preferring to set seed in quantity without the bother of blooming.

Cultivation Ordinary droughtland. Some shade is preferred and these small plants seem inclined to scorch if exposed to much direct sunlight.
Propagation Seed. Not really slow growing. These are very small plants and will not appear to be making much growth when young seedlings.

FREREA (Ascelepiadaceae)

The one species, *Frerea indica*, from eastern India, is now included in *Caralluma*, as *C. frevei*, by some botanists. However, its distinction as the only member of the stapeliads which possesses true leaves and the ease with which it may be grown (rare among Indian asclepiads) should entitle it to keep its greenhouse identity.

Frerea indica grows naturally on steep slopes close to waterfalls. Its bright-green semi-succulent leaves are complemented by small flattish flowers of purple brown, marked with yellow. There is a hybrid of vigorous growth between this species and *Caralluma europaea.*

Cultivation Simple enough. Shade and moisture are the key, with reasonable warmth at all times, as this is a tropical species. In a broad pan *F. indica* is able to grow as it would like to do (in the absence of its native, wet rock faces), making leafy mats of criss-crossing prostrate branches.
Propagation Easy from cuttings, or from seed, if obtainable.

FRITHIA (Mesembryanthemaceae)

This is a monotypic genus, its one species, *F. pulchra*, being superficially like *Fenestraria*, and its manner of growth in the wild very similar. Flowers are solitary and white, or purple and white, and usually appear in spring. Out of flower, these two plants, *Fenestraria* and *Frithia* may easily

Fouquieria fasciculata, one of the Mexican barrel trees, from southern Mexico. Fouquierias are xerophytic shrubs, some of which tend towards succulence and others, like the species illustrated, towards the caudiciform.

be distinguished by those not very familiar with them. *Frithia* is rough to the touch; the stems and 'window' of *Fenestraria* are quite smooth.

Cultivation As for *Fenestraria;* but this species is a spring to summer grower.
Propagation Seed. Cuttings are just possible.

GASTERIA *(Liliaceae)*
A genus of rosette plants from South Africa and Namibia. They are usually stemless and form clumps. All species are at first distichous, with their leaves in two ranks; but most eventually become rosulate. The naming of these plants is still confused and the position is not helped by the fact that many species resemble each other in their juvenile stage. Nevertheless, these are charming plants, with much variety of foliage and attractive hanging bell flowers of red or rose carried on wiry stems. Many fine hybrids exist between gasterias and aloes or gasterias and haworthias, most being produced in Japanese nurseries and now finding their way into European collections. Gasterias and their hybrids all make excellent houseplants, being content to grow in shadier conditions than most succulents.

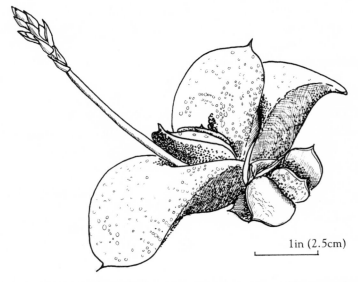

1in (2.5cm)

Gasteria armstrongii, a dwarf species from the eastern Cape Province. The leaves do not grow into a rosette, but remain distichous. The upper surface has a deep depression and is finely tubercled.

Cultivation Droughtland to dry forest. Too much shade will cause plants to become too loose in growth, with pale bases to the leaves, a condition which is easy to notice. Spraying is beneficial, and necessary indoors, to remove dust.

Propagation Easy from seed or offsets. Leaf cuttings, if slower, also offer a good means of increase.

GIBBAEUM *(Mesembryanthemaceae)*
Most gibbaeums come from one part of the Little Karoo, a very arid area whose inhospitable climate is relieved by winter rains. In cultivation these most attractive plants are not among the easier mesems to suit. They will grow well enough, but they prefer not to bloom with any enthusiasm. Probably our northern lack of winter light is largely responsible and it is quite possible that the provision of supplementary lighting to give higher intensities and a longer day might help considerably. However, these are plants with considerable appeal, even out of flower. The bodies of the different species are variously shaped and offer beautiful contrasts of colour and texture. Some species are very highly adapted and others possess longer, paired leaves.

Cultivation As winter growing desert mesems. Bright conditions are necessary to bring out the colour of plant bodies. Gibbaeums should be kept very dry when resting.

Propagation Seed or cuttings.

GLOTTIPHYLLUM *(Mesembryanthemaceae)*
Although most of the species in this genus come from similar habitats to those of the preceding genus, they are much easier to grow and flower. Glottiphyllums have a delightful oddity and are easy to recognise. They seem to grow on their sides, lying prostrate, as if overcome by the heat, their longish, blunt, green leaves extending horizontally. The flowers of *Glottiphyllum* are large and freely produced; they are, with one exception, golden yellow and on a mature specimen may almost hide the foliage.

Cultivation Easy. Plants will take much water when growing, but easily lose character and colour if given more than they strictly need.

Propagation Seed or cuttings, which root easily.

GRAPTOPETALUM *(Crassulaceae)*

A small genus, but a valuable one in the greenhouse; in addition to its own attractive species, there now exist a number of hybrids between these and other genera of the *Crassulaceae*, some with showy flowers.

Graptopetalums come from Mexico and the south-western USA. They are similar to echeverias in growth and habit, but the petals of the flowers are marked with spots or bands. The hybrids with echeverias include some particularly fine cultivars which flower profusely, usually in spring.

Cultivation Droughtland. Very easy, if treated as echeverias; too generous a hand with the watering can will produce lush, colourless and characterless plants, especially if diet (ie food and compost) is also too rich.

Propagation Usually from offsets or leaf cuttings. Species may be increased from seed.

GREENOVIA *(Crassulaceae)*

Very similar to *Aeonium*, but with floral differences. In summer, their resting time, these Canary Island mountain succulents dry up to a small, globular rosette. Flowers are bright yellow in winter or spring.

Cultivation As for aeoniums. Fairly hardy.
Propagation Seed or offset rosettes.

GYMNOCALYCIUM *(Cactaceae)*

South American globular cacti, very variable, and valuable in cultivation for the handsomely spined bodies and free flowering habit. Common to many of the species is a noticeable protuberance, or 'chin' below the areoles. Flowers are borne near the crown; they are large and beautiful and are usually pink or white, or less often red or yellow.

Cultivation Typical droughtland to semi-desert. Not difficult.
Propagation Seed, which usually germinates well.

HAAGEOCEREUS *(Cactaceae)*

A Peruvian genus of erect, sprawling or prostrate cereiform plants, which are sometimes branched. They soon grow into sizeable specimens, to 3ft (1m) high in some species. Flowers are usually white, but not seen on small plants, although these have the advantage of possessing the brightest coloured spines.

Cultivation Droughtland. Easy growers.
Propagation Seed, sometimes cuttings.

HARRISIA (*Cactaceae*)

Quick growing Central American erect or climbing cacti, usually with slender stems. They have charm as young plants, which greatly increases when flowering size is eventually attained, a likelihood which may be greatly increased by planting specimens out into greenhouse beds. When this is done the rate of growth is also increased and one may then begin to expect the large nocturnal white flowers, which may be fragrant. (*Eriocereus* is a synonym for this genus.)

Cultivation Jungle cactus, but warmth needed for most species.
Propagation Seed or cuttings. One or two species are valued as grafting stocks.

HATIORA (*Cactaceae*)

A name now more or less lost in *Rhipsalis*. It is still sometimes seen, however, for one or two species which have an individuality of their own (at least to gardeners). *Hatiora salicornioides*, in its one or more forms, has distinct, bottle-shaped joints of a yellowish green, in whorls of three to five, which make up stems that grow in any direction. This indecision of purpose provides the common name of 'Drunkard's Dream', which name describes a much more charming jungle cactus than might be expected. It has golden-yellow flowers and pale fruits.

Cultivation Easy, jungle cactus. Appreciates spraying.
Propagation Seed or cuttings.

HAWORTHIA (*Liliaceae*)

Probably the most popular succulents in the lily family, with some species known to have been in cultivation for many years. Yet, unfortunately, the ease with which these tolerant plants may be grown and flowered and their acceptance of lower light levels than most other succulents, has often been to their disadvantage. Banished like a naughty child to a dark corner of a room, or half-forgotten under the greenhouse staging, a sad haworthia may linger on for years. But it will give little indication of its real beauty.

Superficially, haworthias are much alike; they are all leaf succulents, from South Africa or Namibia, and all except one or two species grow as rosettes, either singly or in clumps. The flowers of haworthias are also very similar, being racemes or panicles of two-lipped whitish or greenish tubular flowers, very small in size and carried on long, often untidy, wiry stems. In their modest way, haworthia flowers are beautiful miniatures, but this genus is invariably cultivated for the plants themselves. Leaves may be hard or soft, of many shapes and often finished with a lovely translucency or fenestration. Leaf surfaces, too, may be plain, tubercled or marked in a variety of ways, and although most plants may be described as simply green, within this one colour may be found every shade imaginable. Most haworthias are easy to grow – indifferently. It is to bring out the individual beauty which each possesses that skills and care are needed.

The genus *Haworthia* is principally native to South Africa and Namibia, with one or two outlying species. Habitats vary, as do the habits of the individual species. Some, for instance, have developed windows at their leaf tips, like the ones found in some mesems, so that they may grow half-buried in the soil and avoid the harmful effect of extreme sun heat while still benefiting from its light. Some species grow in shaded positions and some prefer exposed ones; some remain green in the wild and others change to various shades of yellow, orange or brown, changes which some specialist growers try to duplicate in their greenhouses.

In recent years the genus has received a great deal of attention, as the result of which a number of well known old names have been changed.

Cultivation This is a genus of trouble-free succulents; at least most of them are. Although in theory subject to the usual pests and diseases, haworthias do not seem to attract them much in practice. They are also fairly hardy if they are not too wet, 40°F (5°C) is safe for them, although it seems best to continue watering all year round. In winter just enough water should be given to keep the compost slightly moist and no more. How much light or shade should be given to a particular species is a matter for experiment and is to some extent dependent upon how the grower prefers his plants to look. Haworthias are co-operative plants. Some species appear to prefer making new growth at one time of the year, some at another. One cannot be dogmatic and specify which do which. Once again, one can only advise experimenting.

Propagation For most haworthias this is easy, as they will make offsets or new rosettes which have only to be detached, rooted (if not already so) and then potted up. Leaf cuttings may be tried for species which do not provide ready progeny, though it is not always easy to keep small leaves in condition until they root. Those species which have hard leaves are the most successful. Sometimes offsets are formed upon flower stems, which root quickly in the propagator. Seed, if viable, will soon produce good specimens, even if some remain small for a while. Seed pods often appear in a collection of haworthias; unfortunately, this is nearly always attributable to cross pollination and any seed should be discarded.

1in (2.5cm)

Haworthia baccata, sometimes considered to be a variant of *H. coarctata*, a species which has a wide distribution in the eastern Cape. It is an easily grown plant, with bright green leaves which are handsomely tubercled.

HESPERALOE *(Liliaceae)*

A small genus from Mexico and Texas; it is sometimes available and not without charm once the edges of the long leathery grooved leaves develop their fibrous edges. The flowers are pink to red, sometimes with a green tinge.

Cultivation Simple droughtland.
Propagation Seed.

HOODIA *(Asclepiadaceae)*

A genus of most distinctive, shrubby plants from South Africa and Namibia, Angola and Bushmanland. The stems which in some species may reach 3ft (1m) or more, are completely covered with sharply spined tubercles and on mature plants flat or cupped flowers are produced in groups at their tops.

Cultivation As for other stapeliads. These plants will take good watering when active, but are very touchy once they begin to rest. Habitat photographs often show majestic flowering clumps of hoodias, standing in an exposed arid position. Seedlings, however, need considerably more shade and protection. Pictures do not show the remains of the thorn bush which invariably sheltered the hoodia seedlings until the ingrates were big and tough enough to kill it off as they overgrew it.
Propagation Seed or cuttings. Seedlings usually grow well and quickly and make good, branched specimens which often reach 12in (30cm) before the inevitable collapse. Grafting on to a tuber of *Ceropegia woodii* or a similar species is not difficult and this will nearly always save a stem which has rotted at its base.

HOYA *(Asclepiadaceae)*

If not all hoyas are succulent, their admirers will not split any hairs over the fact. The flowers and the scent of these lovely climbers, trailers and shrubs, to say nothing of the foliage, qualify them a place in our greenhouses which nothing can fill better.

Hoyas are found in many parts of the East; in China, eastern India, the Far East and Australia. To give the best account of themselves the larger ones, *H. carnosa* and its many varieties and others, need to be planted out in a bed and helped to climb over the greenhouse roof. Even in a 6in (12.5-15cm) pot, good, freely flowering specimens may be raised and enjoyed. The shrubby species, such as *H. bella* make good bench or hanging plants and have the merit of remaining more compact. Hoyas do not object to bright light on their vines and flowers, but prefer to have their roots in cooler shade. Many sorts make good indoor plants if the foliage can be kept clean and sprayed occasionally.

Cultivation Most are not difficult if given forest succulent treatment. Good feeding and a loose, organic compost is essential, particularly for the more rampant sorts. Hoyas should be kept active all the year round and not allowed to dry out too thoroughly in winter, when they will be perfectly safe at 50°F (10°C) – some at considerably lower temperatures.
Propagation From cuttings, although seed of the species is occasionally to be had. Climbing species have an inclination to produce roots at the nodes of well-leaved mature branches, which can be cut into sections (each with its pair of leaves) and rooted. Alternatively, longer sections of branches may be layered by pegging down and then divided once they have rooted. Hoyas will sometimes sulk for a whole season when potted-up as young plants; such behaviour should be patiently endured and, once growth does begin, will be readily forgiven.

HUERNIA *(Asclepiadaceae)*
Short-stemmed clumpers, from South and east Africa and Arabia. These little plants offer the usual stapeliad delights, in exchange for the grower's frustration. Nevertheless, as stapeliads go, most huernias are not too difficult and the beauty of the flowers makes them desirable additions to any succulent collection. Flowers are inclined to be reddish or whitish, a number having a very pale base colour, upon which are flecks, spots or stripes of red to purple. Many flowers are campanulate, the length of the tube varying considerably; others have a gleaming, richly coloured annulus – hence the name 'Life-buoy Huernias' given to the group. *(Huerniopsis* is a small genus, barely distinct from *Huernia.)*

Cultivation As for other stapeliads.
Propagation Seed or cuttings.

IMITARIA *(Mesembryanthemaceae)*
One species, *I. muirii,* which is now found more often in *Gibbaeum* (as *G. nebrownii*). It is extremely succulent and a winter grower, from the Little Karoo. Pink flowers appear in spring.

Cultivation Desert mesem.
Propagation Seed.

IPOMOEA (*Convulvulaceae*)
This genus, better known for its climbers and garden varieties, includes a few true caudiciforms which should be of interest to the specialist. Annual shoots are made and bluish, funnel flowers displayed in summer.

Cultivation Caudiciform
Propagation Seed.

JATROPHA (*Euphorbiaceae*)
In spite of this being a large genus, from a number of tropical and subtropical habitats, including South America, India and Madagascar, few species are seen in cultivation. *J. podagrica* is the one usually grown; it makes a desirable succulent-stemmed bush, with bold, peltate leaves and brilliant-red flowers. Other species should be sought out and some are at last beginning to appear in seed and plant lists.

Cultivation As for euphorbias of similar appearance, ie dry forest, with much moisture when actively growing. When the leaves fall, should be kept almost dry. Not too cold at any time.
Propagation Seed or stem cuttings.

JOVIBARBA (*Crassulaceae*)
Once part of *Sempervivum*, this genus now holds species which have a similar overall appearance, but flowers which are distinct. These, instead of sharing the reddish colour of the larger genus, are yellow or whitish and possess 6-7 petals only, compared with 8-16. They are hardy and very suitable for the garden, and now offer a great variety of forms and cultivars.

Cultivation Droughtland. No heat is needed under glass, but much light is essential to keep growth tight.
Propagation Usually offsets or divisions. Seed is possible.

JUTTADINTERIA (*Mesembryanthemaceae*)
A small genus of small subshrubs and clumpers, from Namibia. They are thick leaved and have flowers of white to purple.

Cultivation Desert mesem. Winter growing.
Propagation Seed.

KALANCHOE *(Crassulaceae)*

A very large genus of well over one hundred species, native to Madagascar (Malagasy Republic), Africa, east India and other parts of the tropical world. Colourful and for the most part easy to grow, they provide the succulent house with some of its loveliest plants and showiest flowers. A few species propagate themselves with such prodigality that they can almost become weeds. But most give no trouble at all in this respect and deserve all our attention.

In habit, kalanchoes range from prostrate to several feet in height. Some are epiphytic and some climbers or scramblers. Foliage varies from smooth to furry and, in colour, from palest green to rich red or purple, in all shapes and sizes. Most species flower readily and display blooms of every shade, including rich dusky browns.

Cultivation As most kalanchoes are native to woodland habitats they appreciate generous treatment. Most of the disappointment which they sometimes bring is caused by the attempt to treat them as terrestrial cacti, a form of abuse which kalanchoes can only repay by dropping most of their leaves and turning into almost dry, woody stems with a few miserable leaves at the top. Rich compost is needed for most of the vigorous species with good watering and feeding for most of the year. General potting is also essential and specimens which are growing well may need to be potted on more than once in a season. Some bottom leaves are bound to drop; but if more than a few fall, the signal is being clearly given that something is amiss. These plants should never, never be allowed to dry right out.

The very small, epiphytic species need more care. They are not as strong growing, although their tastes are similar to those of the larger species. Compost for these miniatures should always be moist, but never wet, and spraying is always appreciated, as it is by the taller sorts.

Many kalanchoes make very excellent houseplants; indeed there is now a whole range of attractive, flowering cultivars, based upon *Kalanchoe blossfeldiana,* and sold in florists' shops for this purpose. Bright, warmish conditions should be given indoors. Too much shade brings poor etiolated growth. In the greenhouse, too much dry heat should be avoided. Given a knowledge of their real nature and needs, the grower should find kalanchoes to be among his most colourful and rewarding plants.

Propagation Cuttings of all sorts are usually very easy and hardly require propagator conditions. Seed is also a simple means of increase.

KEDROSTIS (Cucurbitaceae)

A genus of African caudiciforms which is fairly new to succulent plant collections. *K. africana* is the species most often referred to, but seed of a number of others is now available and all are worth growing. Caudexes are attractive, particularly when young, and the annual vines are fresh and green, with lobed leaves, yellow flowers and pretty fruits which slowly turn from green, through yellow, to red. The vines have tendrils, by which they. are able to cling tightly to any support provided. It is sometimes said that kedrostis species are dioecious, that is, that plants are either male or female. At least one, however, *K. africana* bears both male and female flowers on the same plant, which makes pollination simpler and the production of fruits more likely.

Cultivation Forest treatment. Easy to grow and to flower. If plants are not allowed to dry right out they will often begin their top growth very

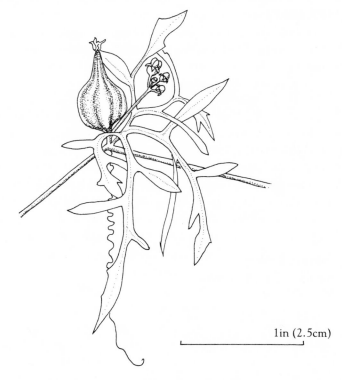

1in (2.5cm)

Kedrostis africana produces a pretty annual vine from a silvery-grey caudex which may grow to a diameter of several inches in time. The flowers are pale yellow and the gourd-like fruit ripens to a deep orange colour.

early in the year and this can then be encouraged by spraying. After fruiting, when the foliage withers, plants should be given a brief, dry period and then the compost slightly moistened and kept so.

Propagation Seed. Top growth does not seem likely to root.

KHADIA *(Mesembryanthemaceae)*
A small genus, close to *Nananthus,* with attractive tapering keeled leaves and flowers of white to purple.

Cultivation Droughtland. Summer growers which rest during spring.
Propagation Seed or cuttings.

KLEINIA *(Compositae)*
See under *Senecio.*

LAMPRANTHUS *(Mesembryanthemaceae)*
A very large genus of free flowering, glabrous subshrubs, easily grown and very colourful if used as garden bedding plants during the warmer months.

Cultivation Easy droughtland mesem.
Propagation Seed or cuttings (which root easily).

LAPIDARIA *(Mesembryanthemaceae)*
One charming species only, *L. margaretae,* from Namibia. It should be grown in a similar fashion to dinteranthus species and should then reveal the true beauty of its highly succulent body, which is much like a semi-precious stone. Flowering takes place in late autumn and the blooms are golden yellow and as much as 2in (5cm) in diameter.

Cultivation Desert mesem.
Propagation Easy to raise from seed.

LENOPHYLLUM *(Crassulaceae)*
A small genus from Mexico and the American Southwest. Close to both *Sedum* and *Echeveria* botanically. Attractive yellow flowers and leaves which are usually brownish in colour.

Cultivation Droughtland.
Propagation Seed or cuttings.

LEUCHTENBERGIA (*Cactaceae*)

The one species (from Mexico) is quite distinctive. *L. principis* grows with a deep taproot and a strong corky stem, which may branch later. Papery three-angled tubercles bear woolly areoles and spines, with large scented flowers of golden yellow.

Cultivation Semi-desert. Needs a deep pot.
Propagation Seed. Easy to raise, but slow growing.

LEWISIA (*Portulacaceae*)

A small genus of easily grown xerophytes, from the western side of the Rocky Mountains. All are rosetted and some species grow stout roots, which are almost caudiciform in appearance and function. Most lewisias are evergreen and produce a number of heads, each of which will flower, in spring. Many hybrids and selected strains are now available and all sorts grow well and flower readily. The remaining species have deciduous leaves; these appear in spring and stemless flowers are borne among them. After flowering, the whole plant dies away, to appear again (if one is lucky) the following year.

All lewisias are hardy and will stand harder winters than are usually experienced in the British Isles. For the garden, the evergreen types are superb, if they are planted so that water does not collect in their rosettes.

Cultivation Easy droughtland plants. The deciduous species need most care, much water when showing above ground, and then an almost dry, long rest.
Propagation Seed. Cuttings for the named varieties.

LITHOPS (*Mesembryanthemaceae*)

These are without a doubt the best known of all the dwarf mesems and it is difficult to resist the admission that they are probably the most colourful and fascinating. The 'Living Stones' or 'Pebble Plants' comprise no more than forty species at most, but forms and varieties of these bring them up to a total of almost one hundred different sorts. Added to this must be the fact that it is frequently difficult, even in one batch of seedlings, to find two plants which are exactly alike. It is no wonder that *Lithops* hold such affection among succulent plant growers.

The genus is spread across the desert areas of Namibia, the Cape Province and reaches into the Transvaal. The plants are highly succulent and consist of no more than one or more pairs of leaves, of varying shape according to the species, but all with a central fissure running across the top, from which the single white or yellow flower grows. In nature the flat, or flattish, top of the plant grows on a level with the surrounding terrain and is coloured to a great extent to suit the colour of its background. In this way, lithops are protected from predators and it is likely that most natural colonies have been found by accident, if they were not seen in flower.

Once one understands the way in which these 'mimicry' mesems grow naturally, it is not particularly difficult to grow and flower them in the greenhouse. Most forms are regularly available from specialist seedsmen and as complete a collection as even the most fanatical collector is likely to achieve can be grown in the space of a few square feet of greenhouse bench.

1in (2.5cm)

1in (2.5cm)

(*above*) Lithops *pseudotruncatella* and (*below*) Lithops *turbiniformis*. Both are easily grown species with yellow flowers.

Cultivation Desert mesem but it is important to observe the natural cycle of growth in order to be successful. The flowers of *Lithops* begin to appear in July or August, and the season extends into November or even later. While plants are actively growing and blooming they will take no harm from being watered and fed freely. As the flowers wither and die, watering should be reduced and then almost completely withheld. One watering from below might be necessary in April or May, to prevent the dying back of the finer roots. During the rest period the plants will dry and shrivel. It is at this time that novice growers are sometimes betrayed by their own love of their plants into killing them with kindness, attempting to water the dried little things back into health. In fact, the plant bodies, when they appear to be dying are behaving exactly as they should be. They are dying, and from their moisture is being produced the pair or double pair of leaves which will be the following season's body.

Lithops are usually quite capable of making their own way into the world when the time comes. The dried skin will crack or split and the new bodies begin to respond to the light and grow. Usually, they are still not in need of water and will not be until they have completely emerged. However, some specialists do like to assist things, either by fine misting (best at evening) or with a little water. This does no harm in most cases, and at least helps the grower through his period of impatience. Lithops are very hardy and need little or no heat during the rest period, especially if winter days are sunny and warm.

Propagation Cuttings may be taken and will root without much trouble. Seed, however, is cheap and an easy way to raise an attractive, varied colony of each species or form.

LOBIVIA *(Cactaceae)*

Probably no other group of plants has been so argued over by the taxonomists as the lobivias and their relatives. It is not unusual to find all the following genera now included in the one genus *Lobivia*. Their names are listed here as a guide to frustrated gardeners who are trying to find plants whose names they thought they knew:— *Acanthocalycium, Acantholobivia, Chamaecereus, Cylindrorebutia, Digitorebutia, Hymenorebutia, Mediolobivia, Pseudolobivia, Soehrensia.*

Cultivation Droughtland to semi-desert. 'Lobivias' are often called be-ginners' plants. Most of the cacti covered by the above list are certainly easy to grow and the flowers, which are often freely produced are colourful and sometimes quite large.

Propagation Again, it should be suggested that most of the above cacti would make a good introduction to raising succulents from seed. They are easy, seed is available for many sorts, and a number will flower when quite young.

MAIHUENIA *(Cactaceae)*

A most interesting, but small genus of high mountain cacti from the Andes. In that hard exposed environment they grow as tight low bushes, their stems rather like those of miniature opuntias – spined and bearing persistent cylindrical leaves. Flowers are opuntia-like, in white, yellow or red.

Cultivation Droughtland. Quite hardy. These tough, little plants would probably survive out of doors in most parts of the British Isles, if they could be kept dry enough. Under glass maihuenias grow well, but always too openly.

Propagation Seed. This always seems to fail in a propagator and is better if given 'alpine' treatment. Sown in early spring, placed out of doors and put into the domestic refrigerator at night if the weather is not cold enough, seed should germinate well. Cuttings root reliably.

MAMMILLARIA *(Cactaceae)*

A very large genus, principally native to Mexico, but with some species found in the American Southwest, the West Indies and South America. For the gardener this is a genus of cacti of almost infinite variety, in size, habit, flowers and spines, not to mention the bright rings of edible fruits which often follow the blooms.

It was to be expected, of course, that such a large and complex genus would act like a jam jar set out for wasps at a picnic and attract the taxonomists. Under *Mammillaria*, a number of re-classified old friends are at present held captive, which were once to be found under such names as *Bartschella, Cochemiea, Dolichothele, Krainzia, Mammillopsis, Phellosperma, Solisia* and even more.

Cultivation Droughtland to semi-desert.
Propagation Seed or cuttings.

MELOCACTUS *(Cactaceae)*
From the warmer parts of Central America, these cacti are globular or cylindrical and some reach a considerable size in habitat. They are distinguished by a woolly cephalium, which gives them the name 'Turk's Cap'. This does not, unfortunately, begin to grow until the plants are quite old. Seedlings, however, do have their own attraction and are well worth growing.

Cultivation Semi-desert to forest.
Propagation Seed.

MESTOKLEMA *(Mesembryanthemaceae)*
A small genus of bushy branched shrubs, with small variously coloured flowers and tuberous roots which have appealed to some caudiciform collectors.

Cultivation Droughtland.
Propagation Seed.

MOMORDICA *(Cucurbitaceae)*
Similar to *Kedrostis,* this is a small genus of interest to caudiciform succulent growers. Unfortunately, only one species seems to have reached collections so far, M. *rostrata,* though undoubtedly others would be worth growing if they were to be had.

Cultivation As for *Kedrostis (qv).*
Propagation Seed.

MONADENIUM *(Euphorbiaceae)*
Among more recent additions to succulent greenhouses the monadeniums rank very high. In many ways these fascinating plants, from east Africa and various regions of tropical and southern Africa, parallel euphorbias in the nature of their different forms. Some species are shrubby or even tree-like and some are caudiciform; nearly all are spineless. As with euphorbias, it is the bracts which are colourful rather than the actual flowers; in some species of *Monadenium* they are quite small, but in others bright and showy.

Cultivation This must depend upon the area from which a particular species comes. Some monadeniums are tropical and others need less heat. Once this basic knowledge is taken into account, these most interesting and usually lovely succulents are not difficult to grow, if treated as similar species from other genera, in particular those of *Euphorbia*. In general, monadeniums need droughtland to dry forest cultivation, always in well-drained porous compost.

Propagation Seed or cuttings. Root cuttings of some species succeed well.

MONANTHES *(Crassulaceae)*

A small genus from the Canary Islands, Madeira and North Africa, mostly perennial and found in various ecological niches, coastal, subalpine, forest and others. These are tiny succulents which grow as shrubs or mats, with foliage which is often a shade of bronze or grey and flowers of quiet colour. Their appeal is not showy, but they are often to be found in the collections of connoisseurs.

Cultivation Moderation should be the key. These are not difficult plants to grow; but they easily grow out of character, or lose their roots if too wet. Sandy soil and not too much water should produce specimens of lovely, miniature beauty.

Propagation Cuttings. Seed, if obtainable.

MONILARIA *(Mesembryanthemaceae)*

A fascinating genus of winter growing Namaqualand shrublets, which one sometimes wishes were easier to grow well and to flower. They are not difficult to keep alive and come readily from seed. The problem with these desirable mesems is that they do not always rush back into growth when the proper time comes. It has been advised that if October comes with no sign of activity, specimens should be encouraged by watering them into life and then continuing to water until flowering ceases. The dormant period should not be too dry. Flowers are white, purplish or red.

Cultivation Desert mesem, but see above.
Propagation Seed. Cuttings are possible.

MONVILLEA *(Cactaceae)*

A genus of a few species, seed or plants of which are sometimes obtainable. The plants are slender climbers from South America, which make vigorous growth and eventually produce beautiful nocturnal flowers.

Cultivation Forest with nourishing compost and free watering when growing well. Never too hot or dry. To grow as they should monvilleas need much room and would be happiest planted out in a bed, from which they could be trained up to the greenhouse roof.
Propagation Seed or cuttings, which root easily.

MOSSIA *(Mesembryanthemaceae)*
One species only, *M. intervallaris* is a dainty, creeping perennial which roots as it goes, with white or cream flowers which open at night. This is a rare and delightful succulent which looks specially well in a small hanging pot, in a position which is slightly shaded.

Cultivation As for other shrubby mesems; in its little way *Mossia intervallaris* is quite vigorous, once established.
Propagation Seed or cuttings.

MUIRIA *(Mesembryanthemaceae)*
An intriguing, monotypic species; even among the mesems, *M. hortensae* is very rare in its habitat so imported wild specimens should be refused. It grows as an extremely succulent pair of leaves, with a fissure so small as to barely separate them, and hardly visible until a flowerbud appears. During the dormant summer season, the old dry skin completely shields the new growth which is being made, as with conophytums.

Cultivation Desert mesem. Grow much as a conophytum, with care.
Propagation Seed is occasionally available, in quantity, and this usually germinates well.

MYRTILLOCACTUS *(Cactaceae)*
These, in their native Mexico, California or Guatemala, grow into much-branched shrubs, up to 10-12ft (4m) high. After flowering, edible fruits are produced which are sometimes sold in local markets. In cultivation flowers are unlikely to appear until plants are very old. Only the one very distinctive species *M. geometrizans* is grown – even as a seedling this possesses a beautiful bluish body.

Cultivation Droughtland. Not difficult.
Propagation Seed and eventually top cuttings.

NANANTHUS *(Mesembryanthemaceae)*
A name for a small genus of plants from the Great Karoo, sometimes combined with *Aloinopsis (qv)*.

NEOHENRICIA *(Mesembryanthemaceae)*
One species only from the centre of the Great Karoo, *N. sibbetti* is proba-bly the smallest of the mesems, growing as a tiny carpet of leaves which have roughened tuberculate tips, similar to some *Titanopsis* species. Per-fectly in scale are the equally miniature, almost white flowers. These open in the evening and have an intensely sweet scent.

Cultivation As for *Titanopsis*. For such a miniature plant it is quite vigor-ous once it is growing contentedly.
Propagation Seed and careful division.

NEOLLOYDIA *(Cactaceae)*
A genus close to *Mammillaria*, which now includes *Cumarinia* and *Gym-nocactus*. They are small terrestrial cacti, with a strong fibrous root system, globular to cylindrical bodies and largish, pink to purple flowers borne at the crown.

Cultivation Droughtland cactus.
Propagation Seed.

NEOPORTERIA *(Cactaceae)*
This is the name under which such genera as *Chileoreburia*, *Horridocac-tus*, *Islaya*, *Neochilenia*, *Pyrrhocactus* and others may now be linked. They are all from South America and are small, terrestrial cacti, not often branching, and bearing flowers which are yellow, pink or reddish.

Cultivation Droughtland. Some species are considered difficult.
Propagation Seed. Seedlings sometimes grow slowly.

NOLINA *(Agavaceae)*
These are really small trees, with strong succulent trunks and a large tuft of long narrow leaves. One or two are seen in collections, where, in a large pot, they make bold specimens. However, they do take up a great deal of space once they get into their stride.

Cultivation Droughtland. Quite easy.
Propagation Seed.

NOPALXOCHIA (Cactaceae)

Small genus close to *Epiphyllum*, with similar flat leaf-like stems which make long hanging growths, and have large pink or red flowers which remain open during the day.

Cultivation Jungle cactus, as for *Epiphyllum*.
Propagation Cuttings or seed.

NOTOCACTUS (Cactaceae)

A genus of South American cacti, spherical to cylindrical, of undoubted beauty. Unfortunately, the genus does not offer the same variety of form or flower as others do, which has lessened its popularity. Nevertheless, there are very desirable species to be found in *Notocactus* and not all flowers are bright yellow, lovely as this can be. The genus now includes *Brasilicactus*, *Eriocactus*, *Malacocarpus* and *Wigginsia*.

Cultivation Droughtland cactus.
Propagation Seed which soon produces attractive specimens.

ODONTOPHORUS (Mesembryanthemaceae)

A small genus of winter growers, from the Cape Province. They grow into attractive clumps and produce yellow or white flowers.

Cultivation Desert mesem, with little water at any time.
Propagation Seed.

OPHTHALMOPHYLLUM (Mesembryanthemaceae)

A small genus of small highly succulent plants, sometimes included in *Conophytum* and resembling either the species of that genus or those in *Lithops*. In nature, these little plants grow buried to their tips; in pots they are safer raised, although they will probably pull themselves down. Flowers are white, pink or purple.

Cultivation Desert mesem. Give long summer rest and not too much water.
Propagation Seed.

OPUNTIA *(Cactaceae)*

An extremely large genus, which includes trees, shrubs, bushes and dwarf forms, and which is spread widely over the Americas, from Canada to Chile. It is even naturalised in parts of the eastern hemisphere. The best known group are the plants with flat joints, which so often form the background in western films, but those which are similar in growth, with cylindrical joints, are also numerous. Both types grow in many sizes, from the tall tree-like species down to those which make prostrate mats, often yards across. Few of these opuntias flower in collections, at least

1in (2.5cm)

Opuntia diademata, a species from Argentina, sometimes seen growing under various names. The joints are brownish-green or grey-green with low warts and large, brownish areoles. The flowers are creamy white and funnel shaped, but the real interest lies in the long, papery spines which are typical of the *Glomerata* group of opuntias.

not those which are growing in pots, although many cactus collectors find their varied forms sufficient as to warrant greenhouse space. Some do flower, and very beautifully, too but the majority need to be planted out in greenhouse beds, so that they can make the growth needed to bring them to maturity and flowering size.

It is surprising that the remaining types of opuntia are seen only in specialist collections. Those which are usually listed as *Tephrocactus* or *Micropuntia* are smaller species, of considerable appeal, but more difficulty. However, their great advantage is that they take up considerably less space in a small greenhouse and may more easily be grown to a flowering size. These small opuntias are not always easy to obtain, but are well worth finding. Even if one must wait for the magnificent flowers, the plants themselves are good enough to be given space.

Cultivation Droughtland treatment will suit most species, large or small. Bright light is always essential but, in nature, the smaller mat-forming sorts are sometimes found growing in light shade. Opuntias like to stretch their roots out, often poking them through the holes in the bottom of their pots and then sending them out to a considerable distance. Mat formers are best grown in flat pans, so that they can root their prostrate chains of joints down into the compost. Some species are almost hardy and can sometimes be grown outside in Great Britain. If such a method of growing is planned, it would be wise to choose a warm protected corner, perhaps against a wall, or to cover plants in winter with something like a light straw covering.

Propagation Seed is sometimes offered, and is a good way of obtaining the rarer smaller sorts. Cuttings of whole pads root reasonably well if dried for a day or so or sealed. Joints sometimes root more quickly if laid flat or stuck sideways into the compost. All opuntias have, if not spines, glochids, which are small tufts of bristles or barbed hair, and these frequently break off in the skin of one's hands. The innocent-looking species are often the worst (*O. microdasys*, for example) and it is always wise to handle any opuntia with gloves on or with a pair of large tongs or tweezers.

OREOCEREUS *(Cactaceae)*

A small genus of lovely, columnar cacti from South America. The stems are covered with long hair, from which, in some species, stout spines protrude. *O. trollii*, perhaps the best known species, has the longest hair and has been called the 'Old Man of the Andes'; it makes a perfect partner for *Cephalocereus senilis*.

Cultivation Droughtland. These cacti are sometimes referred to as being difficult but there seems little reason to agree. Plants raised from seed or cuttings in cultivation grow readily enough and seem resistant to a captive life.
Propagation Seed or cuttings.

OROSTACHYS (*Crassulaceae*)
A small genus of Asiatic succulents, close to *Sedum*. They are monocarpic and form dense clumps of rosettes which flower in their second or third year, producing a tallish spike of white or reddish flowers, packed densely from its top to its bottom. *O. spinosus* is quite hardy in most gardens in the British Isles, if kept dry in winter.

Cultivation Droughtland.
Propagation Seed or cuttings.

OROYA (*Cactaceae*)
Rather individual plants, from South America, which are fairly hardy. They grow, nearly always, as solitary, globular specimens, bearing pink to red flowers near their crown.

Cultivation Droughtland. Perhaps not as easy to grow as well as most terrestrial cacti.
Propagation Seed.

OSCULARIA (*Mesembryanthemaceae*)
A very small genus of easily flowered shrubs from the Cape Province, which make very fine outdoor specimens for the summer. The flowers are pink and small, but borne in abundance in spring. The foliage is a handsomely pale bluish-green, and the small paired leaves carry tiny teeth.

Cultivation Shrubby mesem.
Propagation Seed or cuttings.

OTHONNA (*Compositae*)
A few years ago, one began to see othonnas in quite a number of collec-

tions. Then quite suddenly the interest seemed to flag, hardly any were offered for sale and even those already in cultivation slowly vanished. The only reason for this would seem to be that these intriguing composites would not adapt to our northern seasons and could not find enough enthusiasts to treat them correctly. If this is so, it is a pity; composites are rare in succulent plant collections and othonnas have a distinctive character, even if some species incline towards weediness.

The genus is native to South Africa and Namibia and includes, among its succulent members, leaf succulents and stem or caudiciform succulents, which are quite unlike anything in other genera. The one species which has long been in cultivation, Othonna capensis, is a fairly common, greenhouse plant for hanging baskets. It does not, perhaps, give a very encouraging picture of the genus, although it can look charming, in its way, if starved in good light. Other species, such as O. euphorbioides, O. herrei, O. leptocaulis, and many more are very different, with attractive yellow flowers, bright foliage, spines on occasion and, above all, the striking caudexes which most have. Now that a more reasonable attitude towards succulent plant growing exists, it would be a very good thing for our hobby if othonnas could once again attract attention and show what they have to offer.

Cultivation Semi-desert to droughtland. The difficulty of cultivation which some species have shown in the past is probably due to their being mishandled. Nevertheless, the habitats of some, and their neighbours in those places, would suggest that they need care. Othonnas usually begin to leaf up in late autumn (some earlier), a process which may be hastened by judicious spraying. As the flowers fade, and the leaves begin to yellow, less water should be given and the plants then given a long rest period, during which they should be kept almost dry, until there are once again signs of new leaves appearing.

Propagation Some species lend themselves to increase from stem cuttings, which root easily. Seed is an excellent alternative method, and the only one in some cases. The problem is that seed, however viable it seems to be, can be very obstinate in germinating. It is my experience that whenever othonna seed has germinated, it has done so with perfectly ordinary treatment, although the failures have been as frequent as the successes. From time to time, miracle methods have been put forward but, again in my experience, not one has given consistent results. The mystery is intriguing, more so in view of the facts reported by one

South African seed supplier. Apparently, when he throws away all his unsold succulent plant seed on to a patch of waste ground behind his establishment each year, he sees it come up like grass, along with all the other items.

OXALIS *(Oxalidaceae)*
A large genus, among which a few species, from South America and South Africa offer an individual charm for collections. Alas, it has to be admitted that many others are little more than weeds, if we accept the definition that a weed 'is a plant in the wrong place'. Lovely these things may be but once inside the greenhouse they usually prove themselves the worst of nuisances. Therefore, choose with care. *O. succulenta, O. carnosa* and a few others will give no trouble; other good species are worth finding. Flowers are usually yellow, but colours also include some lovely pinks and dusky reds.

Cultivation Droughtland.
Propagation Seed or cuttings from suitable species.

PACHYCEREUS *(Cactaceae)*
In their Mexican habitat these are giants; in cultivation they become fine specimens for the back of the greenhouse bench, though the growth of some species is slow, those in the wild taking many years to reach maturity.

Cultivation Droughtland to semi-desert.
Propagation Seed.

PACHYCORMUS *(Anacardiaceae)*
Superficially similar to *Bursera microphylla,* this is the famous 'Elephant Trunk Tree', from Baja, California. In a pot this strange-looking succulent grows an oddly-shaped thickened trunk, covered with thin papery peeling bark and, eventually, twisted branches, with small pinnate, deciduous leaves.

Cultivation Droughtland.
Propagation Seed.

PACHYPHYTUM (*Crassculaceae*)
Although this is a small genus only, all its species are worth possessing and its hybrids with *Echeveria*, to which it is close, are equally desirable. Pachyphytums are easy, free flowering, rosette plants, some tall growing and some stemless, with foliage of green or paler shades, covered in some species with a heavy farina. Flowers are hanging and campanulate, with red or white petals.

Cultivation Droughtland rosette, as for *Echeveria*.
Propagation Seed. Leaf or rosette cuttings.

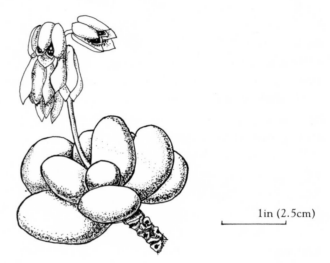

1in (2.5cm)

Pachyphytum oviferum, one of the Mexican rosette succulents. All have attractive leaves and hanging bell flowers, which are sometimes, as in this species, pale-coloured outside and a rich red within. The leaves of P. *oviferum* are pale violet-blue and heavily powdered; its popular name is 'Sugar Almonds'.

PACHYPODIUM (*Apocynaceae*)
South Africa, Namibia and Madagascar (Malagasy Republic) are the principal homes of these beautiful spiny tree or shrub succulents. The leaves are deciduous leathery and green, ovate to long. Flowers are white, yellowish or reddish. The diversity of form among the few species of this genus is enormous and, if they can be obtained, all are worth growing. Fortunately, the trade in imported specimens is declining and nursery propagation is taking over, a situation for which we should all be grateful as these plants, especially the Madagascan species, are not common in the wild.

Cultivation Semi-desert. Some species grow in rock fissures. When growing well, plants may use much water but care is always needed in handling them. Warmth is needed at all times.

Propagation Seed or cuttings for those species which grow in a way which produces suitable material. *Pachypodium succulentum*, an easier species to grow and flower may be increased by root cuttings. Grafting is also used for the more difficult sorts.

PARODIA *(Cactaceae)*

South American terrestrial cacti, small in size and usually solitary and globular. Always popular because of their attractive spines and lovely flowers, which are usually brilliant red or yellow.

Cultivation Droughtland to semi-desert.

Propagation Seed. Seedlings grow slowly at first and therefore need care in their early stages.

PECTINARIA *(Asclepiadaceae)*

A genus (related to *Piaranthus*) from the Cape Province, distinctive among the *Stapeliae* by reason of the fact that the tips of the corolla lobes are joined, giving the flowers a cage-like appearance. Pectinarias grow procumbently or half-buried, their stems often burrowing into the ground.

Cultivation Droughtland. Best in wide pans with deep grit, so that the plants may indulge their preferred way of life.

Propagation Seed, cuttings or divisions.

PEDILANTHUS *(Euphorbiaceae)*

Succulent shrubs from Mexico, California and the West Indies, with unusual euphorbia-like inflorescences, with an irregular cyathium and brilliant red bracts.

Cultivation Droughtland to semi-desert. Not difficult, if given treatment similar to that given to euphorbias from similar environments.

Propagation Cuttings which root readily. Seed, if obtainable.

PELARGONIUM *(Geraniaceae)*

Succulent or xerophytic shrubs, some dwarf and caudiciform, from

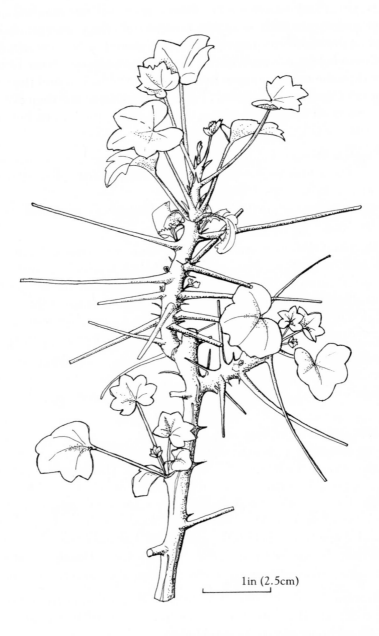

1in (2.5cm)

Pelargonium spinosum, a native of the north-western Cape. It is unique among its fellows because of its long, sharp spinescent petioles. Few of the many pelargonium species are strictly succulent, but they are, nevertheless, very suitable for inclusion in a succulent collection.

South Africa and Namibia. Out of a genus of over two hundred species and many hybrids, both natural and man-made, there are a number well suited to the succulent plant greenhouse, even if only a few species are strictly succulent or caudiciform. Those amateurs who have not seen other than the more common hybrid pelargoniums will find the species remarkable and widely differing, both in their foliage and their zygomorphic flowers, in not only the expected reds, pinks and purple, but also in many other shades, including yellow.

Cultivation Droughtland, dry forest or semi-desert, according to the species. Those from the western side of southern Africa are winter growers and should be treated as such.
Propagation Seed or cuttings, both easy methods for most sorts.

PELECYPHORA (*Cactaceae*)
Very dwarf, usually solitary, cacti from Mexico, which are still rare in cultivation, principally because of their slow growing nature. They are remarkable for their hatchet-shaped tubercles and the appearance of their miniature spines which are arranged in a comb-like fashion. In *P. aselliformis* the spine-clusters resemble a louse. Flowers are purple.

Cultivation Semi-desert to desert. The compost should contain very little humus. Not easy plants.
Propagation Seed or offsets, which are frequently grafted.

PEPEROMIA (*Peperomiaceae*)
A large genus of terrestrial and epiphytic leaf succulents and semi-succulents from the forests of South America. The fleshy leaved 'house plants' are well known; the succulent species much less so. They have an individuality of their own and a fascination for some collectors which is more of an obsession. Most have green leaves but these vary greatly in size and shape. One species, *P. graveolens*, has juicy translucent leaves which have deep-green upper surfaces and are rich red below. A number of these wonderful plants have windowed leaves, like those of some mesems.

Cultivation Tropical forest. Not difficult if given warmth and not too wet a compost. The miniature species like *P. columella* need rather more care. Good house plants, in good light.
Propagation Cuttings or seed. Single leaves will root, but not as readily as one feels they should.

PERESKIA (Cactaceae)

These are true cacti, trees, shrubs or scramblers, which are hardly succulent. They are very spiny, with large, somewhat fleshy, deciduous leaves, only the large woolly and spiny areoles reminding one of cacti. The flowers are single, 2-3in (5-7.5cm) in diameter and may be white, yellow or pink, with fruits to follow.

These are most attractive plants, from tropical America. They need warmth, plenty of food and water when active and, unfortunately, much room. However, they can be enjoyed when smallish and then be grown again from cuttings, which root very easily.

Cultivation Tropical to cool forest.
Propagation Seed or cuttings.

PERESKIOPSIS (Cactaceae)

Very similar to *Pereskia*, but smaller in their parts. Usually seen used as rootstocks for slow growing seedling cacti.

PIARANTHUS (Asclepiadaceae)

A small shade loving genus of small creeping and rooted stapeliads, some of which have short joints and resemble potatoes. The bodies are greenish, but may also be brown, grey or darker, with a greenish tinge. Flowers are small but most attractive, usually hairy and sometimes resembling starfish, in various colours and combinations.

Cultivation Droughtland, but shady. These are among the easier stapeliads.
Propagation Seed or divisions.

PLECTRANTHUS (Labiatae)

Close to *Coleus*, this large genus has some species with fleshy leaves, one or two of which are sometimes seen in collections.

Cultivation Dry forest, or moister.
Propagation Seed or cuttings.

PLEIOSPILOS (Mesembryanthemaceae)

Mesem lovers should count themselves fortunate that the 'Granite Plants' are so easy to grow and flower, in spite of their high degree of succulence. The genus, distributed in the Karoo, the Cape and the Orange Free State, comprises between thirty and forty species, all of which, due to the spotted appearance and the texture of their bodies, resemble granite or stone. They vary much in appearance but all have similar large golden flowers, which have the scent of coconut. *Pleiespilos* are summer growers, another advantage for northern gardeners.

Cultivation Semi-desert to desert. Easy plants to care for. The skill lies in adjusting the amount of light, heat and water given, to bring out the plants' resemblance to stone.
Propagation Seed. Seedlings grow quickly and flower when young.

PLUMERIA *(Apocynaceae)*
The genus is better known in tropical gardens than in the succulent greenhouse. Seed of one species or another is offered occasionally by seedsmen and would be worth trying. *Plumeria* is the Frangipani – shrubs or trees with succulent stems, leathery leaves and large, sweetly scented flowers in panicles.

Cultivation Tropical forest.
Propagation Seed.

POELLNITZIA *(Liliaceae)*
Close to *Astroloba,* or to *Aloe,* depending upon your botanist. One species, which should be cultivated according to the grower's taxonomical allegiance.

PORTULACA *(Portulacaceae)*
Most of this genus is made up of annuals or perennials, which are used for summer bedding schemes. A few however, are worthy of space in the succulent collection and these will be found in specialist seed lists. Flowers are often small and do not readily open.

Cultivation Droughtland with much light.
Propagation Seed or cuttings.

PORTULACARIA *(Portulacaceae)*
One species only from South Africa, which should be in any collection with space for it, the variegated form being particularly valuable. *P. afra*

is a large, succulent shrub with a stem marked at intervals into bands and resembling an elephant's trunk. The leaves are green, roundish and fleshy, and the flowers (hardly ever seen) are tiny and reddish. A specimen of any of the several forms in a large pot is a fine sight.

Cultivation Droughtland to dry forest. Not too cold. Summer grower.
Propagation Cuttings, which should not be kept too wet.

PSAMMOPHORA *(Mesembryanthemaceae)*
Winter growing mesems, from the Namib and the Richtersveld, these small clustering plants are remarkable for the sticky foliage which attracts a coating of sand. The flowers are solitary, in white or violet.

Cultivation Desert mesem.
Propagation Seed. Cuttings are possible.

PTEROCACTUS *(Cactaceae)*
Interesting low growing Mexican and South American plants which grow from a large tuberous root. Succulent cylindrical branches carry terminal flowers of reddish brown or reddish yellow.

Cultivation Semi-desert. Best grown with the root raised, as a caudiciform succulent. Not too wet.
Propagation Seed or cuttings.

PTERODISCUS *(Pedaliaceae)*
A small genus of African caudiciforms still rare in collections, which have attractive foliage of various types and largish bright flowers in several colours.

Cultivation Dry forest, on the warm side.
Propagation Seed or cuttings of top growth.

QUIABENTIA *(Cactaceae)*
A very small genus of tree or bushy cacti, with an appearance similar to *Pereskia* or *Cylindropuntia*. The stems are cylindrical and the leaves are fleshy and more or less persistent. The areoles are large and woolly and spines numerous. Flowers resemble those of *Pereskia* and are reddish.

Cultivation Droughtland to dry forest.
Propagation Seed or cuttings.

RAPHIONACME *(Asclepiadaceae)*
Some of the species of this east African genus are now coming into cultivation. Raphionacmes are tuberous rooted or caudiciform succulents, which in the rainy season produce twining stems of small lanceolate leaves and dainty asclepiad flowers in purple or greenish brown.

Cultivation Droughtland to dry forest.
Propagation Seed.

REBUTIA *(Cactaceae)*
A long popular genus of easily grown, small terrestrial cacti from South America. They have no ribs, but instead possess spirally arranged tubercles, with small spines. Flowers are displayed in profusion in spring, in almost every shade of pink, salmon, orange and red. The genus is now usually taken to include *Aylostera* and *Mediolobivia*. One or two specimens at least are indispensable to any collection deserving of the name.

Cultivation Droughtland with a little shade.
Propagation Seed or offsets. Seedlings may flower when less than eighteen months old.

RHINEPHYLLUM *(Mesembryanthemaceae)*
A genus of approximately a dozen species, mostly from the Karoo. They grow as small shrublets or low tufts, often with attractively marked leaves. The flowers are yellow.

Cultivation Desert mesem.
Propagation Seed or cuttings.

RHIPSALIS *(Cactaceae)*
A wonderful genus of tropical and subtropical, epiphytic, branched shrubs, from many parts of Central and South America (the one or two species in the Old World being probably introduced). Most species grow quickly in moist forest conditions and display an amazing variety of stem shape and size. Flowers are small and usually white to yellow – borne in abundance, as they so often are, they can create a lovely effect, some adding the attraction of a faint sweet perfume. Fruits are smooth and round and are usually white, red or blackish. (*Rhipsalis* now usually includes *Hatiora*, *Lepismium*, *Rhipsalidopsis*, *Pseudozygocactus*, and one or two other names).

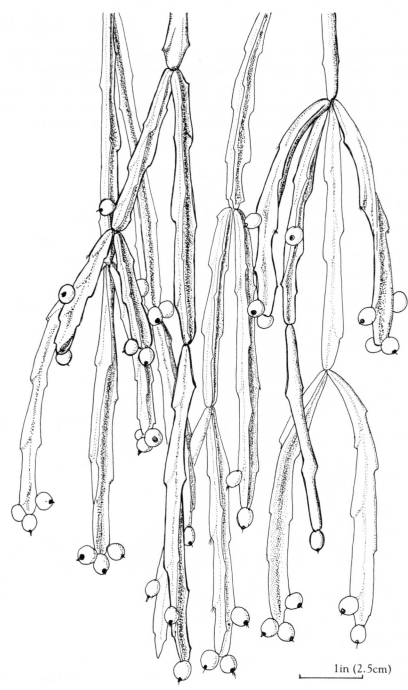

Rhipsalis tonduzii, from Costa Rica, a rain-forest cactus which appreciates a rich compost and humidity. The small, whitish flowers are followed by white berries.

Cultivation Rain forest, although a number of species will stand cooler conditions. Species which are not too large make excellent indoor plants, as long as they are not allowed to become dry. Kitchens and bathrooms, if not too cold, are very suitable. In summer, most rhipsalis appreciate being hung in the shade of orchard trees, or in similar places.
Propagation Seed or cuttings.

RHOMBOPHYLLUM *(Mesembryanthemaceae)*
Very few species, from the eastern Cape, a region with summer rainfall. The leaves are nicely marked and the flowers golden yellow. These attractive mesems are easy and free flowering.

Cultivation Droughtland
Propagation Seed or cuttings.

ROSULARIA *(Crassulaceae)*
This is an Asiatic genus of hardy perennial rosette plants, close to both *Sempervivum* and *Sedum* and sometimes treated as a member of the latter genus. These are attractive plants and would do well in the garden if northern winters were drier. Under glass, much light is essential to prevent plants from drawing up. Flowers are carried in panicles and are usually white, yellow, red or dilute shades of these colours.

Cultivation Droughtland. Quite hardy out of doors, but protection from rain or snow is advisable during winter.
Propagation Seed or offsets.

RUSCHIA *(Mesembryanthemaceae)*
A large genus of well over 300 species which are spread over most of southern Africa. The species vary from large, much-branched shrubs of up to 6ft (2m) or so down to tiny prostrate carpeters. Some are very much like *Lampranthus*, with similar but smaller flowers in various pinks, whites and purples. Most species are easy and the larger ones make fine dry garden plants during summer.

Cultivation Droughtland to desert. Taller shrubby species are native to more eastern areas and prefer growing in summer; the tinies come from further west and should be treated as winter growers and given more care.
Propagation Seed or cuttings.

SANSEVIERIA *(Agavaceae)*

It is a matter for regret that this remarkable genus of African and Indian succulents is so little known in the United Kingdom. Apart from the popular 'Mother-in-Law's Tongue', *S. trifasciata,* and one or two forms of *S. hahnii,* few are seen; yet one North American nursery lists almost 200 sorts and a number of these are common to cultivation in the USA.

Sansevierias take many forms and occur as tall, cylindrical species, small epiphytic ones or in a number of other medium-sized varieties. All are more or less succulent, easy to grow and flower, with a great choice of beautiful foliage (often marked or striped) and are suitable for greenhouse and indoor cultivation. Flowers appear as a panicle of whitish tubes (often sweetly scented) with much nectar, and followed frequently by small fruits. Sansevierias usually form clumps, offsets appearing on tough, underground rhizomes.

Cultivation Droughtland to dry forest. The genus should never be over-fed or overwatered and cannot stand wet stagnant conditions. These are very tough plants which do not mind dry indoor situations and some shade. Low temperatures are not to their liking and 50°F (10°C) is a safe minimum, with perhaps a little less for some species. Do not overpot.
Propagation Seed or offsets. Leaf cuttings are frequently used to good effect but these will not reproduce some colour forms, notably the yellow-margined form of *S. trifasciata.*

SARCOCAULON *(Geraniaceae)*

This genus is xerophytic rather than strictly succulent and it consists of between ten and twenty different species and forms from South Africa and Namibia. All are low, intricately branched, very drought-resistant shrubs, usually spiny and with the stems covered with a resinous coat. They are both desirable and not too easy to obtain. Flowers are radially symmetrical and variously coloured.

Cultivation As for other semi-desert to desert xerophytes and succulents from this area. Winter growing, with leaves which dry and fall to announce the end of the growing season. Then should follow a long, almost dry rest.
Propagation Seed.

SARCOSTEMMA *(Asclepiadaceae)*

A small genus of vining branched succulents from tropical to subtropical Asia, Australia and Africa. They are not common in collections, but are beginning to attract asclepiad specialists. They are worth growing for the beautiful long stems as well as their exquisite flowers, often borne in abundance and usually sweetly scented.

Cultivation Forest, as for similar ceropegias. Much growth may be made during the season, which may be encouraged by generous treatment.
Propagation Seed or cuttings. Easy.

SCELETIUM *(Mesembryanthemaceae)*

An intriguing genus of some twenty species from drier parts of the Cape Province. They are distinctive in appearance, growing as more or less prostrate undershrubs whose leaves die and desiccate without falling, leaving dry, veined, skeletal growth which clothes the stems. Flowers are white or yellowish, pleasant and often scented.

Cultivation Semi-desert or droughtland.
Propagation Seed or cuttings.

SCHLUMBERGERA *(Cactaceae)*

A genus of few species but many cultivars, the species being Brazilian, and the horticultural forms including the popular 'Christmas' cactus and 'Easter' cactus. Most forms grow as thickly branched, spreading shrubs, with segmented stems, which are often toothed. Well grown specimens can eventually reach an impressive size and bear hundreds of zymomorphic blooms in shades of red, purple or white. The genus now includes *Zygocactus* and *Epiphyllanthus*.

Cultivation Not difficult for most cultivars, though the smaller epiphytic species are not so easy to establish. Schlumbergeras dislike strong light and will happily spend most of the year in moist forest conditions under the staging. They like acid compost which is never allowed to dry right out. Limey water is harmful. Flowering usually begins, for the early cultivars, in autumn and a suitable selection of varieties should provide flowers until spring. Sudden changes of light, humidity or temperature may cause buds to drop. Underpotting appears to suit these plants best.
Propagation Seed (for species) or stem cuttings, which should consist of at least two segments and be laid flat to root.

SCHWANTESIA *(Mesembryanthemaceae)*
A genus of about a dozen species from the Cape Province. Winter growers forming clumps or mats of smooth leaves and yellow flowers.

Cultivation Semi-desert to desert mesem.
Propagation Seed or cuttings.

SEDUM *(Crassulaceae)*
Succulent plant lovers should be doubly thankful for this genus of varied
and floriferous plants. Not only is there a colourful choice suitable for
growing under glass, but an even greater selection of hardy garden
species and varieties. In all, the genus *Sedum* includes at least 500
species, distributed across the northern hemisphere, with a few south of

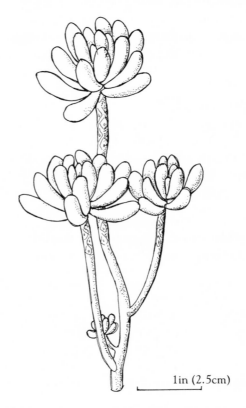

1in (2.5cm)

Sedum pachyphyllum, a strong-growing Mexican species with pale, silvery-green leaves and
bright-yellow flowers. Sedums of this type tend to become leggy in time, but many growers
find the marked stems attractive.

the equator. Here we are concerned only with the non-hardy species, most of which are natives of Mexico.

Sedums are easy to care for and generous with their colour and flowers, even to the beginner. Nearly all are very resistant and several of the commoner ones appear to be quite hardy in an unheated house. They must have very good light if they are to retain their bright colour and not grow out of character, otherwise there is little that can be said about sedums which is not in their favour. The newcomer to succulent growing can indulge himself and collect nearly all of them easily and cheaply, and without qualms.

Cultivation Droughtland. Most sedums are sun lovers. Good light, fresh air and a compost which is on the lean side will produce the most compact, colourful and free flowering specimens.
Propagation For most sorts this is easy. Any leaf will usually root without the need of a propagator. Larger stem cuttings will produce good cuttings more quickly and the beheaded stems should branch rapidly and strongly.

SELENICEREUS *(Cactaceae)*
A genus of climbing forest cacti, often epiphytic in habit and sometimes rampant growing, from the warmer parts of Central America. They are easy to grow although patience will be needed if the beautiful, nocturnal flowers are expected. The famous 'Queen of the Night', *Selenicereus grandiflorus,* is particularly slow to bloom.

Cultivation Warm jungle treatment. Planting out in a bed will produce larger specimens and an earlier chance of flowering.
Propagation Cuttings or seed. Seedlings of most species grow quickly.

SEMPERVIVUM *(Crassulaceae)*
A genus of hardy rosette plants from mountain regions in Europe, Asia and north Africa, which, together with the many hybrids and cultivars, now comprises several hundred sorts. Sempervivums grow into clumps or mats, in a choice of sizes and in nearly all the colours of the rainbow. Flowering is terminal and the flowers, borne on stems, are usually red to purple.

Cultivation These are really plants for the garden. Under glass, with droughtland treatment and very good light, they are deserving of the space which they take up, safe from bird damage and easier to appreciate at close quarters. The hairy sorts also benefit from the freedom from winter wet. No heat is required.

Propagation Offsets or seed.

SENECIO (*Compositae*)

In general, the succulent senecios are winter growers and most prefer not to have to adapt to northern seasons. In fact they will grow for most of the year with a summer rest, but in Britain reserve their best colour and their flowers for colder months. Not that we should grumble; it is a very good thing to have an inducement to visit the greenhouse in wintertime and the senecios will always repay our trouble.

Most succulent senecios come from the African continent, with others native to Madagascar, Mexico and the Canary Islands. Among their particular qualities is the intensely blue foliage of some species and the equally bright silver of others, colours not seen quite as notably elsewhere in the world of succulent plants. Typically composite flowers are carried on a capitulum – (native British groundsels are examples of this sort of inflorescence) and they may be white, yellow, red or even purple in colour. Some flowers are very sweetly and strongly scented.

In form senecios are very varied. Among them may be found examples of leaf, stem and caudiciform succulents. Some species grow into tall, bushy specimens, while others are naturally prostrate but happy to hang as attractive basket specimens.

Cultivation Droughtland to dry forest. Senecios are among the easier succulents to grow. For the winter production of colour and flowers it is helpful to be able to water the plants at this time, so it is safer if they can be kept warmish throughout the colder months – 50°F (10°C) is a suitable minimum although some species will accept less. Bringing plants into the house as an alternative to giving extra heat under glass will be successful only if they can be placed in a very light situation. Without this, senecios quickly grow out of colour and character and flower buds may abort. Drainage is very important as so many species make underground tuber or stem growth. During the rest period plants may be stood down from the bench, in light shade, and kept just ticking over. Once new growth begins, however, they should be placed back in bright light to encourage leaf colour.

Propagation Not difficult for most. Stem cuttings, sometimes already rooted, or divisions take readily. Seed is not often available and is not often set in Great Britain, even when hand pollination is attempted. Nevertheless, both *Senecio spiculosus* and *S. praecox* have self-sown in my greenhouses and have flourished without attention.

1in (2.5cm)

Senecio haworthii, unique among succulents for its stems and leaves which are covered completely in soft, white, felty hairs, giving the common name 'cocoon plant'. The yellow-to-orange flowers are not often seen. *S. haworthii* comes from South Africa, but the exact location is apparently not known.

SEYRIGIA *(Cucurbitaceae)*
A genus which is almost unknown in cultivation, at least in private collections, although its species are worth effort to obtain. *S. humbertii* is usually the one species seen and this makes an effective addition to any collection, growing from tuberous roots into an erect bush of whitely felted climbing stems, with tendrils and (if one is lucky) tiny yellow flow-

ers. Other species scramble about on long stems which are attractively marked.

Cultivation Dry forest, Madagascan treatment seems to suit, with careful watering.
Propagation Seed, if it were obtainable, might succeed. Cuttings root with reasonable success, although those of S. *humbertii* are more difficult.

SINOCRASSULA (*Crassulaceae*)
These are few in number and should be grown like *Sedum* to which they are related.

STAPELIA (*Asclepiadaceae*)
Mostly African, clumping, and close to *Caralluma*, with short upright or semi-prostrate stems, which are sometimes velvety in appearance. The flowers of some stapelias smell of carrion, which they also resemble. Nevertheless, they have a strange unique beauty. They are frequently large (up to 12in [30cm] in diameter) and often fringed and covered with fine silky hair. Insects are attracted by the appearance and smell of these

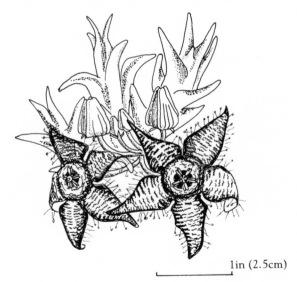

1in (2.5cm)

Stapelia (Orbea) woodii, which is widespread in Natal. It is free-flowering and the fringed blooms are dark reddish-brown, an attractive contrast to the green, toothed stems. In cultivation very good drainage is essential, as it is for all stapeliads.

flowers and blow flies lay their eggs upon them, affecting pollination in the process.

Cultivation Droughtland with some shade. The more vigorous stapeliads are easier to grow and flower. Good drainage is essential.
Propagation Seed or cuttings.

STAPELIANTHUS *(Asclepiadaceae)*
Closely related to *Huernia (qv)* and native to Madagascar (Malagasy Republic).

STAPELIOPSIS *(Asclepiadaceae)*
Related to *Stapelia (qv)*.

STOMATIUM *(Mesembryanthemaceae)*
Small tufted plants of great charm, from the drier areas of the Cape Province. These are summer growers, with solitary scented flowers of white or yellow which open in the evening. Of the forty or so species only a handful are seen very often, but all are worth growing for their flowers and their attractive appearance, not unlike that of dwarf faucarias.

Cultivation Semi-desert mesem. Not difficult.
Propagation Easy from seed or cuttings.

SULCOREBUTIA *(Cactaceae)*
A genus set up as recently as 1951 by Backsberg and now accepted by most botanists. Sulcorebutias are small terrestrial cacti of undoubted appeal and a number are now available to collectors. Most offset to form clumps and the flowers are richly coloured and quite outstanding at times, in reds and yellows, pinks and purples.

Cultivation Droughtland as for *Rebutia (qv)*.
Propagation Seed or offsets.

SYNADENIUM *(Euphorbiaceae)*
East African shrubs or small trees, once classified as *Euphorbia*. All are extremely poisonous but make noble specimens when planted out in large greenhouses. In pots, these large-leaved shrubs make smaller

growth but are worth having as lovely foliage plants. A red form of S. *grantii* is particularly attractive.

Cultivation Dry to moister tropical forest. Not too cold.
Propagation Cuttings. Take care; both latex and plant are toxic.

TACINGA *(Cactaceae)*
Climbing and branching shrubs from North Brazil, with slender cylindrical stems and leaves which are soon deciduous. There are two species at most; they have greenish or reddish flowers, followed by fruits with white seeds.

Cultivation Dry forest.
Propagation Seed or cuttings.

TACITUS *(Crassulaceae)*
As *Tacitus bellus*, this small offsetting Mexican rosette plant caused some excitement among enthusiasts when it was first introduced during the 1970s. Now, reclassified as *Graptopetalum*, it has been allowed to lead a quieter life. It is an attractive plant, close to some echeverias in appearance, and its flowers are brilliantly red on short stems.

Cultivation Droughtland. Easy, as for *Echeveria.*
Propagation Seed or offsets.

TALINUM *(Portulacaceae)*
The species in this genus are little known in collections. The hardier ones from the United States and Canada are sometimes to be found in alpine houses, otherwise few species are ever available. A pity, as some might well prove to be attractive newcomers to our greenhouse benches. *T. guadalupense,* from the Mexican island which gave it its name, can sometimes be obtained. It is a true succulent with a fleshy caudex and grows as a bush up to 28ft (70cm) in height, with pink flowers.

Cultivation Droughtland.
Propagation Seed or cuttings.

TAVARESIA *(Asclepiadaceae)*
This genus of two or three species is widespread in tropical and South Africa. The plants are distinctive in appearance, having a number of ribs

and many stem tubercles, each of which bears bristly spines. Flowers usually appear at the base of the short stems and are very deep throated, in creamy yellow, flecked with reddish purple.

Cultivation Droughtland to semi-desert, with some shade.
Propagation Seed. If rot occurs it is usually possible to root or graft one or more stems.

TEPHROCACTUS *(Cactaceae)*
A name for the dwarfer South American cacti which are now more usually included in *Opuntia (qv)*.

TITANOPSIS *(Mesembryanthemaceae)*
Lovely small winter growers from the Cape and Namibia. The half-dozen or so species have foliage heavily encrusted with whitish tubercles, and grow as thick tufts, with thick rootstocks and yellow flowers.

Cultivation Desert mesem, but much light is needed to keep the growth tight and bring out the beauty of the leaves. Artificial winter light would help greatly. Otherwise, these are not difficult plants to grow successfully.
Propagation Seed.

TRADESCANTIA *(Commelinaceae)*
A genus well known for the many species which make such attractive house plants. One distinctive species, *T. navicularis*, is sufficiently succulent to be accepted into collections. It has small boat-shaped, finely hairy leaves and produces elongated rooting stems on which are borne small mauve flowers.

Cultivation Dry forest or moister.
Propagation Cuttings.

TRICHOCAULON *(Asclepiadaceae)*
A dozen species make up this genus, which is native to the drier parts of South Africa and Namibia. There are two types of Trichocaulon, those with spiny tubercled stems and those without spines. Very small flowers of various colours are produced between the tubercles at the tips of the stems.

Cultivation Droughtland to semi-desert, as for other stapeliads. Not at all easy. Must never be too moist.
Propagation Seed germinates readily. Cuttings root with difficulty.

TRICHODIADEMA (*Mesembryanthemaceae*)
Easy growing small shrubs, widely distributed in southern Africa. They all have fresh green foliage which glistens in the sun and the leaves are tipped with a crown of tiny bristles. Flowers are white, red or purple. These are good succulents for garden use during summer and some species are more or less hardy. One or two other species may be grown as caudiciforms, their tuberous roots making them very suitable for this purpose.

Cultivation Droughtland. Very easily grown.
Propagation Seed or cuttings.

TURBINICARPUS (*Cactaceae*)
A small genus of easily grown dwarf cacti, with prominent spring flowers which may be white, pink, purplish or striped.

Cultivation Droughtland.
Propagation Seedlings may flower at just after one year. These miniatures are not slow growing and flower at a small size.

TYLECODON (*Crassulaceae*)
This name now distinguishes those species formerly in *Cotyledon* which have spirally arranged deciduous leaves and, usually, erect or spreading flowers. The species are winter growing, with thickened stems and sometimes a tree-like growth, although this is not of sufficient size to disqualify them for pot culture. Other species are smaller, even dwarf, in stature. Several are poisonous to cattle in the South African habitats, and this fact should be remembered when any are handled.

Cultivation Droughtland.
Propagation Seed or stem cuttings.

UEBELMANNIA (*Cactaceae*)
A very small genus of Brazilian cacti which enjoyed a fashionable spell in the late 1970s when they began to be imported in quantity, but which

are now seen less often. They are smallish, globular cacti of distinctive appearance – multi-ribbed, with areoles which resemble crests and fine bristle-like spines. *U. pectinifera* is very striking, with its rough stem and white scales. Flowers in this genus are yellow.

Cultivation Droughtland.
Propagation Seed.

VANHEERDEA *(Mesembryanthemaceae)*
Four species only, from the drier areas of Bushmanland. Vanheerdeas resemble the gibbaeums, but have yellow bracteate flowers.

Cultivation Desert mesem.
Propagation Seed.

VANZIJLIA *(Mesembryanthemaceae)*
Not often seen in cultivation, these are low, creeping shrubs from near the sea in the south-western Cape. Plants have two kinds of leaf pairs and white to pink flowers.

Cultivation Droughtland.
Propagation Seed.

VILLADIA *(Crassulaceae)*
Related to *Sedum*, from which they differ in some floral characteristics, these are quite attractive small Mexican and Andean shrubs, with white, yellow or reddish flowers. Not many species are seen in cultivation; others might be well worth introducing.

Cultivation Droughtland. Fairly hardy.
Propagation Seed or cuttings.

WEBEROCEREUS *(Cactaceae)*
Attractive, epiphytic, jungle cacti from Central America. They resemble *Epiphyllum* in their stems and have smaller white or pink flowers, which sometimes have a very sharp, citrous smell.

Cultivation Rain forest, like Epiphyllum.
Propagation Seed or cuttings.

WILCOXIA *(Cactaceae)*
Unusual and interesting climbers from Mexico and lower California. The stems are very thin and sprawling and grow from tuber-like roots. The flowers are brilliantly coloured in pink or red, with green stigmas.

Cultivation Dry forest or droughtland.
Propagation Seed or cuttings.

XEROSICYOS *(Cucurbitaceae)*
Small branching and scrambling shrubs from Madagascar, with very fleshy, round or oval green leaves on thin cylindrical stems. Plants are dioecious and the tiny flowers whitish.

Cultivation Dry forest, Madagascan.
Propagation Cuttings.

YUCCA *(Agavaceae)*
Not strictly succulent, but sufficiently so for some species and forms to be included in trade lists and in collections. Yuccas really need the warmth of mild counties to grow to flowering size in the garden but small specimens in pots can also give great pleasure.

Cultivation Droughtland. Most are fairly hardy.
Propagation Seed.

ZEUKTOPHYLLUM *(Mesembryanthemaceae)*
A small shrub, woody-stemmed and densely leafy, and growing to about 4in (10cm) high. The foliage is greenish with a purple flush and the flowers are yellowish-pink. Hardly ever seen in cultivation.

Cultivation Droughtland probably.
Propagation Seed. Cuttings might root.

Glossary

Actinmorphic (of flowers) Capable of bisection into equal halves (cf zygomorphic).

Adventitious Describes roots which do not arise from the radicle, but from a different part of the plant, usually the stem. May also be used to describe buds which arise from a part of a plant which is not the axil of a leaf.

Annulus The part of the corolla which grows as a fleshy, raised ring in some Stapeliads.

Areole The spine cushion of a cactus.

Bract A modified leaf which is part of an inflorescence.

Bracteole A small bract.

Cactus A plant which belongs to the family *Cactaceae*. The word should not be used, as it sometimes is, for other types of succulent.

Capitulum Used for a flower head which has a number of small flowers growing at the same level and so forming a flat plane.

Capsule A dry fruit, which in suitable conditions will open to liberate its seeds.

Caudex An enlarged storage organ at soil level. It may be either a swollen stem or root or, sometimes, a combination of both.

Caudiciform Possessing a caudex.

Ciliate Fringed with hairs, as are the flowers of some members of the Stapeliae.

Cleistogamous Capable of setting viable seed without the flowers opening.

Cristate In succulent plants, growth which is fasciated or fan-like.

Cultivar A cultivated variety; a plant form which originates in cultivation.

Cyathium The inflorescence of a member of the *Euphorbiae*.

Decumbent Flat growing, but with ascending tips.

Dioecious Having male and female flowers on separate plants.

Distichous Growing in two ranks or series, which are usually opposite.

Diurnal Growing or occurring during daytime.

Endemic Native to a certain place, usually an island or country.

Epicactus A hybrid cactus derived from epiphytic genera and usually possessing large, showy flowers.

Epiphyte A plant which grows upon another, but which is not parasitic in its nature.

Etiolation A condition which arises in a plant grown in insufficient light. The lack of chlorophyll causes a loss of colour and there is a tendency for stems to lengthen between nodes and leaves to grow smaller.

Family A taxonomic grouping of genera with shared characteristics. Family names usually end in -aceae.

Farinose Having a powdery or floury appearance.

Fasciation Abnormal growth which shows as a flattening of part of the plant, usually the stem.

Genus A taxonomic group of related species, sometimes containing one species only.

Geophyte A plant which stores food underground, and which has perennial buds below the surface of the soil.

Glochid The barbed hair or bristle often found in *Opuntia* species.

Habitat The environment in which an organism grows.

Halophyte A plant of maritime situations which has a tolerance of salt. Most species have a tendency towards succulence.

Inflorescence The flowering shoot which carries the flower of a plant.

Internode The part of a stem between two nodes.

Keel The longitudinal ridge on the reverse side of a leaf.

Latex In succulent plants this is a white, milky fluid, which is typically found in *Euphorbia* species and in some members of the *Asclepiadaceae*. It is sometimes poisonous, occasionally very much so.

Mesophyte A plant which lives in environments where the supply of water is an average amount (cf xerophyte).

Monocarpic A plant which flowers only once, at the end of its life.

Monoecious Having both male and female flowers on the same plant.

Monotypic A genus which contains only one species.

Monstrous (of succulents) Having an abnormal form which arises from multiple points of growth.

Node The part of the stem from which the leaves grow.

Panicle A compound inflorescence, whose main stem bears lateral racemes or spikes of flowers.

Papilla A tiny, soft protuberance.

Pedicel The stalk of an individual flower.

Peduncle The stalk of an inflorescence.

Petiole The stalk of a leaf.

pH The symbol used to express the amount of acidity or alkalinity of a solution. In the case of a soil solution, a pH of 7 is considered 'neutral'.

Raceme An inflorescence with a single axis, which bears a number of flowers on short pedicels.

Rhizome An underground stem which assists in vegetative reproduction.

Rosulate In the form of a rosette.

Section A subdivision of a genus.

Shrub A perennial plant which has several woody stems growing from the same root.

Species The basic unit of classification, the group of plants whose members bear the greatest resemblance to each other.

Spine A hard, pointed outgrowth from a stem, which is the result of modification of a leaf, stipule or petiole.

Station One of the precise locations, within a habitat, where a particular species is found.

Stolon A horizontally growing stem or branch which roots at the nodes.

Stoma A breathing pore, in the epidermis of plants (pl stomata).

Subshrub A small shrub, much of whose growth tends to be soft wooded.

Succulent Capable of storing water in specially enlarged tissues. Also a plant of this sort.

Sucker A shoot from the parent plant which originates below the level of the ground.

Taxonomy The science of classification of organisms, including nomenclature.

Tree A woody, perennial plant which usually has a single trunk crowned with a head of branches. 'Tree' succulents (eg some crassulas and aeoniums) are called thus because their overall habit is similar.

Tubercle A small, knob-like outgrowth on a stem or leaf.

Variegation Irregular variation in colour of leaves, flowers or stems, due to the suppression of pigment development in some localised areas.

Vascular bundle Plant tissue which conducts water and food materials through plants.

Xerophyte A plant adapted to survive on less water than average.

Zygomorphic Capable of being divided equally in one plane only, the two halves being mirror-images of each other. The flowers of *Schlumbergera* are typically zygomorphic.

Further Reading

General Books

Rowley, Gordon *The Illustrated Encyclopedia of Succulent Plants* Salamander (1978). One of the very best general reference books. A coffee-table volume, with a text for the intelligent beginner and the experienced grower. Now remaindered, but copies can still be found.

Jacobsen, H. *Lexicon of Succulent Plants* Blandford (1977). A good, general reference to the non-cacti.

Stearn, William T. *Botanical Latin* David & Charles (1973). Quite indispensable and very thorough.

Benson, L. *The Cacti of the United States and Canada* Stamford University Press (1982). Represents the author's life's work. Valuable for the cactus enthusiast.

Specialised Books

Court, Doreen *Succulent Flora of Southern Africa* Balkema, Rotterdam (1981). Comprehensive and knowledgeable, and written by a South African who has practical field experience. Well illustrated.

Pilbeam, John *Mammillaria, A Collector's Guide (1981) and Haworthia and Astroloba, A Collector's Guide* Batsford (1983). Two excellent guides to two popular genera. Fully illustrated.

Evans, Ronald L. *Handbook of Cultivated Sedums* Science Reviews Ltd (1983). A very fine, illustrated work, which is the result of many years of patient and devoted study on the part of the author. (All the hardy species are also included.)

Many other reference books can be obtained and the Public Library Service is invaluable in this respect. Impulse buyers should beware of titles similar to 'Cacti and Succulents'. In most cases such books will give very limited attention to non-cacti.

Whitestone Gardens Ltd, Sutton-under-Whitestonecliffe, Thirsk, North Yorkshire, YO7 2PZ, England, issue a very comprehensive list of books on all aspects of succulent plant study and cultivation, in English and other languages.

Societies and Journals

The British Cactus and Succulent Society, 23 Linden Leas, West Wickham, Kent, BR4 0SE.
(Members receive a quarterly journal. Most attention is given to the terrestrial cacti.)

The International Asclepiad Society, 10 Moorside Terrace, Drighlington, Bradford, BD11 1HX
(The journal gives very good coverage of the *Aslepiadaceae* and its annual seed list is excellent.)

The Epiphytic Plant Study Group, 1 Belvidere Park, Great Crosby, Merseyside, L23 0SP
(A quarterly journal is sent out, which concerns itself with all epiphytic succulents, but principally with those belonging to the *Cactaceae.*)

The Xerophyte, Barleyfield, Southburgh, Thetford, Norfolk.
(The only English language quarterly journal, which gives coverage of the whole succulent plant world, without a bias towards cacti.)

Sources of Supply

Selections of the easier, and often more colourful succulents now find their way into florists and garden centres. Others may be found at cactus nurseries, which often advertise in the gardening press. At these establishments cacti usually take pride of place and it is wise to telephone before making what may be a fruit-less journey. The best sources of succulent plants are not, unfortunately, found in Great Britain. The author has had good specimens and excellent service from the following nurseries in the USA. (If writing to them it is essential to include an International Reply Coupon.)

Grigsby Cactus Gardens, 2354 Bella Vista Drive, Vista, CA 92083, USA
    (Very comprehensive)
Abbey Garden, 4620 Carpinteria Avenue, Carpinteria, CA 93013, USA
    (Also good)
California Epi Center, PO Box 1431, Vista, CA 92083, USA
    (A wonderful source of jungle cacti, in many varieties)

The expense and bother of importing plants are lessened if a small group of en-thusiasts makes up a joint order.
An easier way of obtaining good plants, and rare ones, is to use the service pro-vided by the International Succulent Institute. This is a non-profitmaking or-ganisation which publishes an annual list. Plants ordered are sent out by the British Agent, to whom payment may be made in Sterling.
Apply to: N. E. Wilbraham, 7 Marlborough Drive, Macclesfield, Cheshire, SK10, 2JK, enclosing a foolscap, stamped and addressed envelope.
Also, a very varied catalogue of seeds may be had from Southwest Seeds, 200 Spring Road, Kempston, Bedfordshire, MK42 8ND; and the International Asclepiad Society has an excellent seed list (see Further Reading).

Index